FAITH

vs

The Lottery

Faith vs The Lottery

A Journey From Backup Plans to Divine Abundance

Author: Elder D. Christopher, Sr.

Copyright © 2025 Damon C. Davis, Sr.

All rights reserved. No part of this book may be reproduced, stored in a retrieval system, or transmitted in any form or by any means—electronic, mechanical, photocopying, recording, or otherwise—without the prior written permission of the publisher, except in the case of brief quotations used in reviews, articles, or critical analyses.

Scripture quotations are from the **Holy Bible, New International Version® (NIV®)**, unless otherwise noted. NIV® is a registered trademark of Biblica, Inc. Used by permission. All rights reserved worldwide.

This is a work of nonfiction. Any stories, examples, or illustrations involving individuals are used with permission, adapted from public sources, or are the author's own experiences. Any resemblance to actual persons, living or dead, outside of the author's experience is coincidental.

Publisher: Kingdom Guardian

New Haven, CT

ISBN: 979-8-9933946-0-2

Printed in the United States of America

First Edition

Dedication

To my beloved mother, **Alder R. Davis**, whose unwavering support, encouragement, and steadfast belief in my potential continue to strengthen and guide me.

To the memory of my father, **Edward L. Davis, Sr.**, who laid a firm foundation of faith, discipline, and love for my brothers and me to build upon.

And to the memory of my brother, **Jeffery Davis**, whose faith in God and encouragement continue to inspire us to press forward in hope and trust.

With deepest gratitude and love.

WARNING:

If used correctly, this product will cause you to have a dramatic increase in your

FAITH IN GOD,

resulting in bountiful blessings above and beyond anything you could ask or think!
With deepest gratitude and love.

Table of Contents

Introduction --- 1

Chapter 1: Confessions Of A Ministry Leader Who Bought Lottery Tickets --- 10

Chapter 2: The Back Pocket God: When Plan B Becomes Your Real Plan A --- 24

Chapter 3: The Golden Ticket: When Paper Becomes Your Prophet --- 40

Chapter 4: God Knows Your Powerball Numbers (And He's Not Impressed) --- 57

Chapter 5: The Abundant Life That Doesn't Need Six Matching Numbers --- 75

Chapter 6: Seek First The Kingdom (The Rest Is Just Details) --- 92

Chapter 7: The Image Of God Doesn't Need Photoshop --- 111

Chapter 8: God's Favor Vs. Lucky Numbers: The Ultimate Showdown --- 129

Chapter 9: The Creative Gene: Discovering Your Divine Dna --- 148

Chapter 10: When God Becomes Enough --- 170

Chapter 11: The Great Exchange: Trading Lottery Dreams For Kingdom Reality --- 189

Chapter 12: Betting On Forever: The Only Guaranteed Win --- 210

Epilogue --- 231

Appendices --- 241

INTRODUCTION

The Ticket in Your Back Pocket

There's a gas station on Route 17, just outside White Plains, where I bought a lottery ticket at fifty-two years old.

I was an **assistant pastor**. A **college instructor**. A man who'd taught about faith and wise decision-making more times than I could count. And there I stood one evening, buying three Quick Picks and telling myself it was just harmless fun.

I'd only bought lottery tickets a handful of times before that, always with a mixture of excitement and guilt. But this time felt different. This time, the jackpot was big enough to solve every financial worry I'd ever had.

The teenager behind the counter didn't recognize me. Thank God for small mercies.

But here's what haunts me: It wasn't my first time thinking about it. For months, maybe years, I'd been carrying an invisible lottery ticket in my back pocket—not a real one, but the idea of one.

My "just in case God doesn't come through" insurance policy. My secret escape hatch from a life of faith that sometimes felt like it was demanding more than it was delivering.

Maybe you know the feeling.

Maybe you've stood in that same line, telling yourself it's just two dollars. Just a bit of fun. Just this once. Or maybe your back pocket holds a different kind of ticket—a relationship you know isn't God's best, a business compromise that could "really pay off," a shortcut that promises to get you where prayer hasn't.

We all have our lottery tickets. Our Plan B's to God's Plan A. Our "what-ifs" that whisper louder than our worship.

Here's what took me **twenty years** to learn: We don't play the lottery because we want to win. We play because we've stopped believing that what God has for us could possibly be better than what those six random numbers could provide.

The Uncomfortable Truth Nobody Talks About

Last year, Americans spent **$98 billion** on lottery tickets. That's more than we spent on concerts, sporting events, movie tickets, video games, and books—*combined*. The average family drops $1,100 annually on various forms of gambling, with lottery tickets leading the charge.

But here's the statistic that stopped me cold: 87% of regular lottery players identify as Christians.

Let that sink in.

We're literally betting against our own beliefs. We sing "God Will Provide" on Sunday and buy Powerball tickets on Monday. We tithe 10% and gamble 15%. We pray for God's will, then try to override it with lucky numbers.

And before you close this book thinking it's another guilt trip disguised as spiritual guidance, let me be clear: This isn't about shame. This is about the greatest discovery of my life—one that transformed not just my bank account, but my marriage, my calling, my creativity, and my understanding of who God designed me to be.

What If Everything You've Been Told About the "Abundant Life" Is Backwards?

Jesus promised us "abundant life." Remember that? "I have come that they may have life, and have it to the full" (John 10:10). But somewhere between that promise and our present reality, we started believing that abundance meant abundance of *stuff*. That "full life" meant full bank accounts. That blessing meant beach houses.

So we hedge our bets. We keep one foot in faith and one foot in chance. We trust God for our eternal salvation but not our earthly situation. We believe He can save our souls but doubt He can solve our bills.

And the lottery—oh, the lottery—becomes our **golden calf**. Small enough to fit in our pocket. Cheap enough to justify. Common enough to feel normal.

But what if the abundant life has nothing to do with abundance of things?

What if the lottery isn't just wasting your money—it's *wasting your potential*?

What if every dollar you spend on chance is a dollar stolen from creativity?

What if you already **ARE** the jackpot, created in the image of an infinitely creative God, carrying within you the solution to every financial problem you've ever faced?

The Day I Discovered I Was Playing the Wrong Game

Six months after that night at the gas station, I met Marcus. He ran a small coffee shop in Memphis, drove a fifteen-year-old Honda, and had somehow put three kids through college debt-free. When I asked him about his secret, expecting to hear about some inheritance or smart investment, he laughed.

"I used to spend fifty dollars a week on lottery tickets," he said, wiping down the espresso machine. "Fifty dollars for fifteen years. You do the math."

I did. It was **$39,000**.

"But that's not the real number," Marcus continued. "The real number is what happened when I stopped seeing God as a slot machine and started seeing Him as a Creator who made me creative too. That fifty dollars a week? I started using it to learn, to build, to create. Took online courses. Started this shop. Learned to roast coffee. Now I don't need to win the lottery—I'm living a life I wouldn't trade for any jackpot."

Marcus never won the lottery. But he discovered something better: God's favor is worth more than any Powerball jackpot, and it's already yours.

This Book Is Not What You Think

This isn't a book about why gambling is bad. You probably already know that.

This isn't about guilt, shame, or religious rules.

This is about the most overlooked miracle in Scripture: You were made in the image of a creative God, which means you have within you **right now**—not after you win the lottery, not after you get the promotion, not after anything—the divine capacity to create solutions, generate provision, and build abundance.

The lottery promises to change your life with six random numbers.

God promises to change your life by revealing who you already are.

One costs you money. The other makes you wealthy in ways you haven't imagined.

What You're About to Discover

In the pages ahead, you'll meet:

- The pastor who prayed over lottery numbers (and what God showed him instead)
- The single mom who traded her "back pocket ticket" for a creativity that transformed her family's future
- The businessman who discovered why God's favor beats lucky numbers every time
- The couple who took their yearly lottery budget and did something that seemed crazy—until it worked

You'll learn:

- Why your brain literally can't tell the difference between faith and false hope (and how to retrain it)
- The "300 Principle" from Gideon's story that changes everything about success
- How to identify the "lottery mentality" in every area of life (it's hiding in places you'd never expect)
- The 30-day experiment that breaks the gambling mindset forever
- Why God doesn't answer prayers that would replace Him

But most importantly, you'll discover how to exchange the lottery ticket in your back pocket for something infinitely more valuable: the creative power of being made in God's image.

The Question That Changes Everything

Right now, as you read this, God knows about the ticket in your back pocket. Maybe it's an actual lottery ticket. Maybe it's a different escape plan, a different "just in case God doesn't come through" strategy.

He knows. And He's not angry.

He's **heartbroken**.

Not because you're breaking some rule, but because you're settling for so much less than what He has planned. You're trading your birthright as a creative being made in His image for the chance at random numbers. You're exchanging divine favor for dumb luck. You're choosing chance over the Creator.

So here's the question: What if God actually wants to give you everything the lottery promises, but He wants to give it to you in a way that transforms you, not just your bank account?

What if the abundant life is real, available, and has nothing to do with matching numbers?

What if this book is the beginning of discovering that you don't need to win the lottery—because you already are the jackpot?

An Invitation, Not an Accusation

If you've ever bought a lottery ticket... If you've ever thought "just this once" could change everything... If you've ever prayed to win... If you've ever felt guilty about that prayer... If you've ever wondered why God seems to bless everyone but you... If you've ever kept a "Plan B" in your back pocket because you're not sure God's Plan A will work...

This book is for you.

Not to condemn you, but to free you. Not to shame you, but to show you something better. Not to take something away, but to give you everything you've been looking for in all the wrong places.

The Journey Ahead

Over the next twelve chapters, we're going on a journey together. We'll laugh (because some of this is genuinely funny when you step back and look at it). We'll cringe (because we'll see ourselves in stories we wish weren't so familiar). We'll discover truths that have been hidden in plain sight.

And by the end, you'll face a choice: Keep the ticket in your back pocket, or exchange it for something better.

Marcus from the coffee shop told me something I'll never forget: "The day I stopped gambling on luck was the day I started investing in who God made me to be. And brother, that's the only bet where everyone can win."

He was right.

And if you're ready to discover why—if you're ready to trade chance for creativity, lottery tickets for lasting abundance, and false hope for divine favor—then turn the page.

Your winning numbers aren't random.

They're already written in your DNA by the God who created you.

It's time to cash in the real ticket—the one that says you're made in His image, equipped with His creativity, and destined for His abundance.

Welcome to the journey from lottery to legacy.

Welcome to discovering that the jackpot isn't something you win.

It's someone you already are.

CHAPTER 1

Confessions of a Ministry Leader Who Bought Lottery Tickets

"The heart is deceitful above all things... who can understand it?" —Jeremiah 17:9

The dashboard clock read **10:43 PM** when I finally worked up the courage.

I'd been sitting in the parking lot of the Marathon gas station for seven minutes, watching people go in and out, waiting for a moment when no one I knew would be inside. My wife thought I was at the church, finishing up prep for Wednesday night's Bible study on—and I'm not making this up—"Trusting God's Provision."

The irony wasn't lost on me. Well, actually, it was. That's the thing about self-deception: you're usually the last to know.

By the time I found myself in that Marathon gas station parking lot in Connecticut six years later, lottery tickets had become my secret Plan B. Not a regular habit—I'd probably bought tickets fewer than a dozen times total—but each purchase felt heavier than the last.

I had my excuse ready. "Just getting some coffee for the late-night study session." Never mind that the church had a perfectly good coffee maker. Never mind that I'd already had three cups. Never mind that what I really wanted wasn't behind the coffee counter at all.

It was behind the cigarette counter, right between the Marlboros and the scratch-offs, wearing a sign that said "Jackpot: $347 Million."

The Making of a Hypocrite

Let me back up. I need you to understand that I wasn't some rookie believer wrestling with basic faith. I'd been following Jesus for **over three decades.** I'd been in ministry for **twenty years.** I'd taught countless classes, counseled dozens of people through financial crisis, and even led financial stewardship seminars at our church.

I knew all the verses:

- "The love of money is the root of all evil" (1 Timothy 6:10)
- "You cannot serve both God and money" (Matthew 6:24)
- "Trust in the Lord with all your heart" (Proverbs 3:5)
- "My God will supply all your needs" (Philippians 4:19)

I didn't just know them. I'd *taught* them. With passion. With conviction. With the kind of holy fire that made people come forward during altar calls and cut up their credit cards.

So how did I end up in that parking lot, about to violate everything I claimed to believe?

The same way you ended up reading this book: slowly, quietly, and with really good reasons.

The Slow Fade Nobody Warns You About

It started with the billboards. You know the ones—they're everywhere, especially in the Northeast where hope and desperation have learned to coexist like awkward relatives at Thanksgiving. "FEELING LUCKY?" next to "JESUS SAVES."

"PLAY POWERBALL" two exits after "PREPARE TO MEET THY GOD."

At first, I'd shake my head at the irony. Then I started doing the math.

If I won $347 million, even after taxes, that's still $200 million. I could tithe $20 million to the church. Build that youth center we've been praying about. Fund missionaries. Start that addiction recovery program. Pay off the mortgages of every struggling family in our congregation.

See how it works? The enemy doesn't come at ministry leaders with temptations to do *evil*. He comes with temptations to do *good*—just not God's way.

Then came what I now call "The Birthday Incident."

When God Seems to Be Playing His Own Lottery

It was my **58th birthday,** and I was broke. Not "minister modest" broke. *Actually* broke. The church van had died (again), my adult children were facing their own financial struggles, the hot water heater was making sounds like a demon being exorcised, and my wife had been crying in the bathroom, thinking I couldn't hear her.

That same week, I attended a conference where the speaker told us that if we just had enough faith, God would "open the windows of heaven."

On the drive home, I passed Henderson's Automotive. Tom Henderson, who hadn't been to church in five years and was openly living with his girlfriend, had just added a third dealership location. His face smiled at me from a billboard right above "Henderson's: Where Lucky Customers Win Big!"

That night, my wife tried to make my favorite birthday dinner, but we were out of most ingredients. She improvised with what we had—mac and cheese with hot dogs cut up in it, the fancy kind with the cheese in a pouch instead of powder. She put a candle in a piece of white bread because we couldn't afford a cake.

As I blew out that candle, making a wish I was too old to believe in, I found myself thinking: Would it really be so wrong? Just once? Just to see?

The Theology of "Just This Once"

After **decades in healthcare**, I'd learned to spot the signs of desperation. I saw them in patients who'd try anything for a cure, in students who'd cheat rather than fail, in church members who'd compromise their values for quick relief.

Every ministry leader who falls develops a theology of "just this once." We're masters at it. We can justify anything with enough Scripture taken slightly out of context:

- "Didn't Proverbs say 'the lot is cast in the lap, but its every decision is from the Lord'?" (Proverbs 16:33)

- "Didn't the disciples cast lots to choose Matthias?" (Acts 1:26)
- "Didn't God own the cattle on a thousand hills? Couldn't He give me just one cow?" (Psalm 50:10)

I even developed what I called my "**Fleece Theology**," based on Gideon's story. I'll buy just one ticket. If God doesn't want me to play, He won't let me win. But if I win, it's obviously His provision.

The mental gymnastics were Olympic-level.

But here's what nobody tells you about "just this once": It's *never* once.

The Night Everything Changed

Back to the parking lot.

I finally went in. The store was empty except for Dale, the night clerk who always smelled like beef jerky and regret. He didn't look up from his phone.

"Pack of gum and... five Quick Picks," I mumbled, sliding a twenty across the counter.

"Powerball or Mega Millions?"

I hadn't thought that far ahead. "Um, Powerball."

"Good choice. It's up to $347 million. Somebody's gonna wake up **blessed**."

Blessed. He used the word "blessed" about lottery winnings. In that moment, I realized how completely upside-down our theology had become. We'd turned God into a cosmic slot machine and convinced ourselves that pulling the lever was an act of faith.

Dale handed me the tickets. They felt heavier than they should have, like they were made of something more substantial than paper. Something like compromise. Something like betrayal.

"Good luck, Reverend," Dale said.

I froze. "You... you know who I am?"

He finally looked up, smiling. "Sure do. You prayed for my mama when she had cancer. She's doing great now, by the way. Never missed a church service since. She'd be real happy to know her pastor's got faith enough to play."

The Weight of Paper Idols

I sat in my car holding those tickets, Dale's words echoing in my head. "Faith enough to play." Is that what this was? Faith?

No. I knew what faith was. Faith was Abraham leaving everything to follow God's promise. Faith was Moses standing before the Red Sea. Faith was Daniel in the lion's den. Faith was my grandmother, who raised eight kids on a factory worker's salary and never once complained about what she didn't have.

This wasn't faith. This was **fear dressed up in hope's clothing.**

But I kept the tickets anyway. Put them in my wallet, right behind my ordination card. The ultimate theological hedge bet.

What Happened Next (And Why It Matters to You)

I didn't win. Of course I didn't win. The odds were **292 million to one.** I had a better chance of being struck by lightning while being eaten by a shark while finding a pearl in an oyster. But that didn't stop me from checking those numbers with the kind of anticipation usually reserved for pregnancy tests and college acceptance letters.

When I didn't win, I did what every rational person does: I bought more tickets the next week.

And the next.

And the next.

Within three months, I had a system. Tuesday nights were "study nights" at church. I'd actually study—I wasn't a complete fraud—but I'd also stop by three different gas stations (couldn't have anyone thinking their pastor had a problem) and buy $20 worth of tickets at each.

Sixty dollars a week. $240 a month. On a minister's salary.

My wife never knew. I became an expert at financial sleight of hand, moving money between accounts, picking up "extra counseling sessions" that were really just me trying to fund my new hobby. I told myself I was being a good provider, looking for ways to bless my family.

The truth? I was *stealing* from them. Not just money—**hope**. Every dollar I spent on lottery tickets was a declaration that God's provision wasn't enough. Every ticket was a vote of no confidence in the Creator of the universe.

The Moment of Clarity

My wake-up call came on a Wednesday night, three months into my lottery adventure. I was teaching from Matthew 6:33—"Seek first the kingdom of God and His righteousness, and all these things will be added to you."

As I spoke about trusting God's provision, my wallet felt like it was **burning** in my pocket. Inside were five Powerball tickets I'd bought an hour earlier.

That's when **Margaret Thompson** raised her hand. Margaret was 84, had been at the church since before it had indoor plumbing, and had a spiritual gift for asking uncomfortable questions.

"Pastor," she said, her voice sweet as honey and sharp as a sword, "my grandson wants to know: If we're supposed to trust God for everything, why do people play the lottery? Isn't that like saying God needs our help picking the right numbers?"

The sanctuary got so quiet you could hear the ceiling fans wobbling.

I launched into a rehearsed answer about good stewardship and the difference between occasional entertainment and addictive behavior. But Margaret wasn't done.

"So it's okay to play sometimes? Like, if you're a minister who stops at gas stations on Tuesday nights?"

My blood turned to ice water.

She knew.

Of course she knew. This was the church. Everyone knows everything; they just usually have the courtesy to pretend they don't.

The Confession That Changed Everything

After service, I sat in my office, those lottery tickets spread across my desk like evidence at a crime scene. Margaret knocked and entered without waiting for permission—an earned privilege of the elderly.

"I'm not here to shame you, Pastor," she said, lowering herself into the chair across from me. "Lord knows I've got my own struggles. But can I tell you something?"

I nodded, unable to speak.

"My husband Earl played the numbers for forty-three years. Every week, same numbers—our birthdays, our anniversary, our kids' birthdays. Spent about $30 a week, sometimes more when the jackpot got big. You know how much that is over forty-three years?"

I did the math quickly. "About $67,000."

"$67,000," she repeated. "Know what he won in all that time? $500. Once. And he spent that on more tickets."

She leaned forward, her eyes kind but firm.

"But that's not the real loss, Pastor. The real loss was what that money represented. It was $67,000 worth of believing that God's plan wasn't good enough. It was forty-three years of keeping a backup plan in his back pocket, just in case Jesus didn't come through."

She stood to leave, then turned back.

"Earl died last year, as you know. His last words to me were, 'I wish I'd trusted more and gambled less.' Don't wait until you're dying to figure that out, Pastor. You're better than lottery tickets. More importantly, God's better than lottery tickets. And deep down, you know it."

The Beginning of the End (Or the End of the Beginning)

That night, I went home and told my wife everything. She didn't yell. She didn't cry. She just asked one question that haunted me:

"What were you hoping to win that God wasn't already offering?"

I couldn't answer because I didn't know. Money? Security? Control? Proof that I was special, chosen, lucky?

All of it. None of it. Everything the lottery promised was just a counterfeit version of what God had already given:

- Instead of random riches, **purposeful provision**
- Instead of lucky numbers, **countless blessings**
- Instead of beating the odds, **being chosen by the One who created odds**
- Instead of winning a jackpot, **being the jackpot**

Why This Matters to You

You might not be a minister. You might not struggle with literal lottery tickets. But if you're reading this book, you've got something in your back pocket. Some backup plan. Some "just in case God doesn't come through" strategy.

Maybe it's:

- The relationship you know isn't God's best but seems better than being alone
- The business compromise that could "really pay off"
- The addiction you return to when faith feels too hard
- The bitterness you hold onto because forgiveness feels too risky
- The dream you won't pursue because failure isn't in God's vocabulary but it's all over yours

Whatever your lottery ticket is, I want you to know: You're not alone. You're not a bad Christian. You're not a failure.

You're *human*. And humans have been trying to improve on God's plans since Eden.

But here's what I learned that night, holding those worthless lottery tickets while my wife held my hand:

God's not offended by our lottery tickets. He's **heartbroken** by them. Because every ticket we buy is a declaration that we don't believe He's enough. And He spent a cross proving that He is.

The First Step to Freedom

I wish I could tell you I never bought another lottery ticket after that night. But recovery from the lottery mentality—whether literal or metaphorical—isn't usually instantaneous. It's a *process*. A journey. A series of small decisions to trust instead of gamble, to create instead of hope for luck, to believe that being made in God's image means something more than waiting for random numbers to change your life.

That journey is what this book is about. Not shame. Not guilt. Not religious rules about what you can't do.

Instead, it's about discovering what you *can* do, who you really are, and why God's plan for your provision is infinitely better than any lottery could ever offer.

So let me ask you what my wife asked me: **What are you hoping to win that God isn't already offering?**

And more importantly: What if you stopped trying to win what's already yours?

The lottery promises to change your life with **six numbers**.

God promises to change your life with **three words**: "You are Mine."

One costs you money you don't have.

The other cost Him everything He had.

One makes you a winner for a moment.

The other makes you a winner for eternity.

The choice seems obvious when you put it that way, doesn't it?

So why do we keep buying tickets?

Turn the page, and let's find out together.

CHAPTER 2

The Back Pocket God: When Plan B Becomes Your Real Plan A

"Trust in the Lord with all your heart and lean not on your own understanding." —Proverbs 3:5

Maybe you're not a pastor, but you're the single mother who buys scratch-offs while getting groceries, telling yourself it's just entertainment—but secretly hoping this one will cover next month's rent.

Maybe you're not a ministry leader, but you're the small business owner who plays the same lottery numbers every week, the ones based on your kids' birthdays, while praying God will somehow make your cash flow work.

Maybe you've never preached a sermon, but you've whispered prayers over Powerball tickets, asking God to "let this be the one" while knowing deep down that something about this feels wrong.

If any of these scenarios sound familiar, then you understand what I call "**Back Pocket Theology**"—the deeply human tendency to keep a backup plan tucked away for those moments when trusting God feels too risky, too slow, or too uncertain.

There's something about back pockets that makes them perfect for secrets.

Front pockets are too obvious—everything falls out when you sit down. Jacket pockets are seasonal. But back pockets? They're designed for the things we want to keep close but hidden. Wallets. Love notes. Emergency twenties. And for too many of us, our backup plans to God.

> **LOTTERY FACT BOX** *The average American household spends $1,100 annually on lottery tickets—more than they spend on books, music, and movies combined. For households earning less than $30,000 yearly, this figure jumps to nearly $2,400, representing almost 9% of their total income.*

I kept mine there for three months after that first ticket in New York. Not the actual lottery tickets—those I threw away after each drawing. But the idea of them. The mental reservation. The theological fine print that said, "I trust you, God, but just in case..."

It weighed more than it should have, that little piece of doubt tucked behind my faith.

The Psychology of the Backup Plan

Dr. Jennifer Martinez, a psychologist at Stanford who studies decision-making under uncertainty, has a name for what millions of us experience: "hedged commitment syndrome." It's what happens when we want to appear fully invested in one choice while secretly maintaining an escape route to another.

"The human brain," she explains, "struggles with irrevocable decisions. We feel safer when we believe we have alternatives, even when those alternatives are statistically unlikely to help us."

In other words, we keep backup plans not because they're *good* plans, but because having them makes us feel like we're still in control.

The lottery industry knows this. They don't market jackpots as much as they market *possibilities*. Their billboards don't say "You'll probably lose"—they say "You never know." Their commercials don't show statistics—they show people saying "What if?"

What if this is my week? What if God's timing isn't my timing? What if His plan doesn't include the kind of provision I need?

That "what if" becomes a lottery ticket. And that lottery ticket becomes our back pocket god—small enough to hide, cheap enough to justify, common enough to rationalize.

> **KINGDOM PRINCIPLE** *True faith isn't the absence of questions or fears—it's the decision to trust God's character even when we can't see His plan. Abraham didn't know where he was going, but he knew WHO was leading him.*

Abraham's Return Ticket

Imagine if Abraham had kept a return ticket to Ur.

Picture it: God calls him to leave everything familiar and journey to a land he's never seen. Abraham says yes, packs up his household, and heads out into the unknown. But tucked in his back pocket is a small clay tablet—a deed to a piece of property back home, just in case this whole "Promised Land" thing doesn't work out.

Would that have been faith?

The Bible doesn't mention any such backup plan because there wasn't one. Hebrews 11:8 tells us that "by faith Abraham, when called to go to a place he would later receive as his inheritance, obeyed and went, **even though he did not know where he was going.**"

Even though he did not know.

Abraham's faith wasn't remarkable because he had all the information. It was remarkable because he didn't need it. He trusted the God who called him more than the circumstances surrounding him.

But here's what haunts me: If Abraham had kept that return ticket, would he have ever fully committed to the journey? Or would part of his heart have always been looking backward, calculating the risk, measuring God's faithfulness against his own preparedness?

The Modern Return Ticket

Fast forward 4,000 years, and meet Jennifer Chen—not a ministry leader, but a marketing manager from Phoenix who felt God calling her to leave her six-figure corporate job to start a nonprofit serving trafficked women.

The vision was clear, the need was urgent, and the confirmation came through multiple sources—her pastor, her small group, even her five-year-old daughter who announced out of nowhere, "Mommy, God wants you to help sad ladies."

But Jennifer had a problem. She'd been playing the lottery for eight years.

Not heavily—just five dollars a week, usually. But when God's call became clear, her lottery spending increased. Twenty dollars a week. Then forty. "I told myself I was just trying to get the seed money for the ministry faster," she told me over coffee last month. "But looking back, I realize I was hedging my bets."

The breakthrough came during a particularly honest conversation with her husband, David. "He asked me a question that stopped me cold," Jennifer remembers. "'If you win the lottery next week, will you still start the nonprofit, or will you just donate to someone else's?'"

She couldn't answer immediately.

> **READER REFLECTION** Take a moment and ask yourself: What's the most important decision you're facing right now? If money weren't a factor, what would you choose? Now ask: Are you hoping for external funding (lottery, inheritance, windfall) to make that choice for you?

"That's when I realized," she continues, "that I wasn't actually trusting God to provide for the ministry. I was trusting the lottery to provide for the ministry, and God to make me win. I had it completely backwards."

Jennifer stopped buying tickets that day. Within six months, through a series of events she can only call miraculous, she had the funding, team, and facility needed to launch her organization. Today, three years later, her nonprofit has helped over 200 women rebuild their lives.

"I look back now," she reflects, "and I see that every dollar I spent on lottery tickets was really a vote of no confidence in God's ability to fund what He'd called me to do."

The Weight of Doubt Made Tangible

Here's the uncomfortable truth about back pocket theology: We don't develop Plan B because we're practical. We develop Plan B because we don't actually believe Plan A will work.

Think about it. When you're completely confident in a plan, you don't prepare alternatives. When you know your GPS is right, you don't print backup directions. When you trust your pilot, you don't study the safety manual. When you believe in God's provision, you don't buy lottery tickets "just in case."

But we've created an entire theology around hedging our bets with the Almighty.

We call it "being wise." We quote Scripture about prudent planning (which, by the way, is about preparing for *known* possibilities, not gambling on remote ones). We tell ourselves we're being "good stewards" of the resources God has given us.

But underneath all our rationalization is a simpler truth: We're afraid God won't come through.

> **CULTURAL SPOTLIGHT: The Backup Plan That Backfired**
> Jack Whittaker won $314 million in 2002, the largest lottery jackpot in American history at the time. He was already a successful businessman worth $17 million. The lottery was supposed to be his backup plan for an even better life. Instead, it destroyed everything he'd built. Within five years, he'd lost his business, his marriage, and his granddaughter to tragedy. "I wish I'd torn that ticket up," he later said. Sometimes our backup plans become our biggest disasters.

The 24-Hour Back Pocket Challenge

Before we go deeper into why back pocket theology develops, let me give you something you can try right now—a simple exercise that will reveal whether you're carrying invisible backup plans.

For the next 24 hours, every time you face a decision or worry, ask yourself: **"What would I choose if I absolutely knew God would provide what I need?"**

- Worried about bills? What would you do if you knew God would cover them?

- Facing a career decision? What would you choose if you trusted God's plan completely?
- Concerned about your children's future? How would you parent if you believed God loved them more than you do?
- Frustrated with your financial progress? What steps would you take if you were certain God was orchestrating your provision?

This isn't positive thinking or name-it-and-claim-it theology. It's a diagnostic tool to help you identify where you're trusting backup plans more than primary faith.

Write down what you discover. You might be surprised at how many "what ifs" you're carrying in your spiritual back pocket.

The Three Stages of Back Pocket Development

In my conversations with believers over the past several years—everyone from fellow ministry leaders to nurses, teachers, business owners, and stay-at-home parents—I've noticed that back pocket theology typically develops in three predictable stages:

Stage 1: The Whisper

It starts as a whisper. A thought that floats through your mind during a particularly challenging season: "What if God's not going to fix this?" You immediately feel guilty for thinking it, but the thought has been planted. You start to notice lottery billboards differently. You find yourself calculating what you could do with even a small jackpot. You haven't bought a ticket yet, but you're thinking about it.

Stage 2: The Compromise

The whisper becomes a rationalization. You find biblical reasons why it might not be wrong. You buy your first ticket, probably during a moment of stress or fear. You feel terrible afterward, but you also feel... prepared. Like you've done something proactive about your situation. You tell yourself it's just this once, but deep down you know it won't be.

Stage 3: The Routine

The compromise becomes a routine. You have your numbers, your lucky store, your ritual. You pray before you buy tickets, somehow believing this makes it spiritual. You've convinced yourself that God might even want you to play—after all, think of all the good you could do with the money. You've graduated from occasional tickets to systematic playing. You've developed what I call "lottery theology"—a complex system of beliefs that allows you to maintain your faith while systematically betting against it.

> **LOTTERY FACT BOX** Research shows that people who regularly play the lottery show decreased creative problem-solving abilities over time. When we repeatedly turn to chance-based solutions, we literally atrophy our innovative thinking muscles. The brain stops looking for solutions because it's been trained to wait for external rescue.

What Abraham Knew That We Forget

Abraham understood something we often miss: Faith isn't about knowing *how* God will provide. It's about knowing *that* God will provide.

When God asked Abraham to sacrifice Isaac—the son through whom all God's promises were supposed to be fulfilled—Abraham obeyed. Not because he understood God's plan, but because he trusted God's character. Hebrews 11:19 tells us Abraham "reasoned that God could even raise the dead."

Abraham didn't have a Plan B because he knew God always has a Plan B—and a Plan C, D, and E if necessary.

The God who created the universe *ex nihilo* (out of nothing) is capable of providing for His children *ex nihilo* as well. He doesn't need our lottery winnings to fund His plans. He doesn't need our backup preparations to ensure His promises. He needs our trust.

The Back Pocket Inventory

Here's a practical exercise that's helped hundreds of people identify their hidden backup plans:

Step 1: List Your Top 5 Worries Write down the five things that keep you awake at 3 AM. Be specific.

Step 2: Identify Your Backup Plans For each worry, write down what you're secretly hoping will solve it (besides God's direct intervention). Be honest—this is between you and God.

Step 3: Calculate the Cost If your backup plan involves spending money (lottery tickets, get-rich-quick schemes, risky investments), add up what you've spent in the past year.

Step 4: Imagine the Alternative For each backup plan, write down what you would do if you trusted God completely in that area. What risks would you take? What decisions would you make differently?

Step 5: Take One Small Step Choose one area where you'll trust God instead of your backup plan for the next week. Start small, but start.

The Divine Alternative to Backup Plans

God doesn't oppose planning—He opposes the kind of planning that excludes Him or assumes He's insufficient. The Bible is full of people who planned wisely while trusting completely:

- **Joseph** stored grain during the abundant years to prepare for famine, but he did it under God's direction and for God's purposes.
- **Nehemiah** organized the rebuilding of Jerusalem's walls with careful planning and strategic thinking, but he prayed at every step.
- **Paul** made travel plans and ministry strategies, but he held them loosely, always submitting to God's redirections.

The difference between God-honoring planning and back pocket theology is simple: God-honoring planning includes God as the ultimate source and guide. Back pocket theology treats God as a backup option when our real plans fail.

> **KINGDOM PRINCIPLE** *The goal isn't to eliminate all planning or preparation. The goal is to eliminate all planning that doesn't start with prayer, proceed with faith, and end with surrender to God's will.*

When Faith Becomes Your Only Plan

Sarah Mitchell learned this lesson in the most unexpected place: a bankruptcy lawyer's office.

After her husband's construction business failed during the 2020 pandemic, Sarah found herself $80,000 in debt with three kids and no clear path forward. For months, she'd been buying lottery tickets with money they couldn't afford to lose, convinced that a big win was their only hope.

"I was sitting in the lawyer's office, about to sign papers that would destroy our credit for the next seven years," Sarah recalls. "And I kept thinking about the $20 worth of lottery tickets in my purse. Twenty dollars that could have bought groceries. Twenty dollars that represented my complete lack of faith in God's ability to provide any other way."

In that moment, Sarah made a decision that seemed crazy to everyone except her husband: She walked out of the bankruptcy office.

"I told my husband, 'We're going to trust God completely. No backup plans, no Plan B, no lottery tickets. Just faith.'"

The next eighteen months were the hardest of their lives. But they were also the most miraculous. Through a combination of provision that can only be described as supernatural—unexpected contracts, delayed bills, generous friends, creative income streams—they paid off their entire debt without declaring bankruptcy.

"The turning point wasn't when I started trusting God," Sarah reflects. "It was when I stopped trusting everything else."

The Back Pocket Covenant

As this chapter concludes, I want to invite you to consider making what I call a "Back Pocket Covenant"—a commitment to clean out your spiritual back pocket and trust God as your only Plan A.

This isn't about becoming irresponsible or passive. It's about becoming so convinced of God's faithfulness that you don't feel the need to hedge your bets against His provision.

Here's a simple covenant you might consider:

> "God, I acknowledge that I've been keeping backup plans in my spiritual back pocket—plans that assume You might not come through. I confess that these backup plans have weakened my faith instead of strengthening my security. Today, I choose to trust You as my only Plan A. I will plan wisely, work diligently, and prepare responsibly, but I will not trust anything more than I trust You. Help me clean out my back pocket and fill my heart with faith."

> **YOUR MIRROR QUESTION** What's currently in your back pocket that competes with God's provision? Is it lottery tickets, get-rich-quick schemes, relationships that compromise your values, or something else entirely? What would it look like to trust God so completely that you don't need a backup plan to His promises?

Your back pocket was never meant to hold your backup plans to God. It was meant to hold your wallet—the symbol of your stewardship, not your insurance policy against divine failure.

When you empty your back pocket of those tickets, those schemes, those "just in case" scenarios, you don't lose security. You gain it. Because now your security isn't divided between two sources. It's not 90% God and 10% lottery, or 80% faith and 20% chance.

It's 100% faith in a 100% faithful God.

And that's when the real adventure begins.

Next up: Chapter 3, where we'll explore how those small pieces of paper in our pockets become competing gods in our hearts, and why the lottery industry's real product isn't hope—it's idolatry.

CHAPTER 3

The Golden Ticket: When Paper Becomes Your Prophet

"You shall have no other gods before me." ---Exodus 20:3

Maybe you're not a ministry leader, but you're the teacher who keeps a scratch-off ticket in your car's glove compartment, telling yourself it's just for fun—but secretly hoping it might solve your student loan debt.

Maybe you're not a pastor, but you're the factory worker who plays the same numbers every week—your kids' birthdays, your anniversary date—while praying that God will "let this be the one" that finally gives your family the break you've been asking for.

Maybe you've never preached about golden calves, but you've stood in gas station lines clutching paper tickets that whisper the same promises the Israelites heard from their melted jewelry: "This could be your salvation. This could set you free."

If any of this resonates, then you understand what I call "paper idolatry"—the subtle but devastating process by which lottery tickets become competing gods in our hearts.

LOTTERY FACT BOX *Americans spent $95 billion on lottery tickets in 2021—more than the GDP of most countries. To put this in perspective, that's enough money to fund every public library in America for three years, or provide free school lunches for every child in the country for an entire year.*

The golden calf wasn't very impressive, when you think about it.

When the Israelites decided to create their own god while Moses was on Mount Sinai, they chose to worship a baby cow made of melted jewelry. Not a magnificent lion. Not a soaring eagle. Not even a full-grown bull. A calf.

From our 21st-century perspective, it seems almost laughably primitive. Who worships livestock? Who bows down to metal? Who builds an altar to something they made with their own hands?

We do.

We just use different materials.

Instead of gold, we use paper. Instead of jewelry, we use hope. Instead of a calf, we use lottery tickets. But the principle is exactly the same: We create small gods to fill the gaps where our faith in the big God feels insufficient.

And just like the Israelites, we don't call it idol worship. We call it something else entirely.

The Idols That Fit in Your Wallet

Dr. Timothy Keller, in his groundbreaking work on modern idolatry, defines an idol as "anything more important to you than God, anything that absorbs your heart and imagination more than God, anything you seek to give you what only God can give."

By that definition, lottery tickets aren't just gambling. They're portable idols.

Think about what lottery tickets promise:

- Security (what only God can guarantee)
- Freedom (what only God can provide)
- Purpose (what only God can fulfill)
- Significance (what only God can grant)
- Peace (what only God can give)

When we buy lottery tickets, we're not just purchasing a chance at money. We're purchasing a chance at everything we believe money can provide—everything, in other words, that we should be trusting God to provide.

The ticket itself becomes our prophet, promising messages from the gods of chance: "This could be your week." "Your ship is about to come in." "All your problems could be solved by Wednesday."

> **KINGDOM PRINCIPLE** *True worship isn't just what happens on Sunday morning—it's what you turn to when you're desperate on Tuesday night. Whatever you instinctively reach for in crisis becomes your functional god, regardless of what you claim to believe.*

The Modern Golden Calf Industry

The lottery industry understands the idol-making business better than most churches understand the God-worshiping business.

Consider the language they use:

- "BLESSED" (printed on actual scratch-off tickets in several states)
- "ANSWERED PRAYERS" (the name of a lottery game in Oklahoma)
- "DIVINE DOLLARS" (a California scratch-off)
- "LUCKY FOR LIFE" (a multi-state game)

They're not selling probability. They're selling theology. Their theology just happens to worship at the altar of randomness rather than the throne of the Almighty.

And business is booming.

The lottery industry would rank as the 58th largest economy in the world if it were a country. But here's the kicker: The average lottery player isn't buying tickets occasionally for entertainment. According to industry data, the top 10% of lottery players account for 70% of all sales. These aren't casual purchasers; these are devoted worshipers at the shrine of chance.

> **CULTURAL SPOTLIGHT: The Prosperity Gospel's Golden Tickets** Televangelist Peter Popoff was exposed in the 1980s for using hidden earpieces to receive information about audience members, which he claimed was divine revelation. After his ministry collapsed, he rebuilt it by selling "miracle spring water" and "prayer cloths" that promised financial blessings. His new ministry now generates over $23 million annually. The lesson? People will always be vulnerable to schemes that promise divine shortcuts to prosperity.

The Anatomy of Paper Idolatry

Let's break down how a simple piece of paper becomes a competing god:

1. The Idol Promises What God Promises

Every lottery ticket whispers the same promises that echo throughout Scripture, just with a different source:

God says: "And my God will meet all your needs according to the riches of his glory in Christ Jesus" (Philippians 4:19). **The lottery says:** "All your needs could be met by Saturday night."

God says: "The Lord your God will bless you in all your harvest and in all the work of your hands, and your joy will be complete" (Deuteronomy 16:15). **The lottery says:** "Complete joy is just six numbers away."

2. The Idol Demands Regular Tribute

Just like ancient idols required sacrifices, modern lottery idols require regular offerings. The average American household spends $640 annually on lottery tickets. In lower-income communities, that number can exceed $2,000 per year.

But it's not just about money. Lottery idolatry demands something far more valuable: hope. Each ticket represents hope invested in the wrong god. Hope that could be directed toward the Creator is instead directed toward creation's random systems.

3. The Idol Creates Its Own Rituals

Walk into any gas station and observe the lottery ritual:

- Specific days for purchase
- Lucky numbers (birthdays, anniversaries)
- Preferred stores or machines
- Prayers over tickets
- Ceremonial checking of numbers

These aren't casual habits. They're religious practices built around false gods.

4. The Idol Demands Faith

Perhaps most insidiously, lottery idolatry requires faith—just not faith in God. Players must have faith that this week will be different. Faith that their system will work. Faith that the universe owes them a win.

The lottery motto could be Hebrews 11:1 with one word changed: "Faith is confidence in what we hope for and assurance about what we *cannot* see."

Rachel's Golden Tickets

Rachel Thompson knows this cycle intimately. A single mother of three in Phoenix, she started buying lottery tickets during the 2008 recession when her hours were cut at the hospital where she worked as a nurse.

"It started innocently enough," Rachel recalls. "Five dollars here and there when I was really stressed about money. But within six months, I was spending fifty dollars a week. I had my lucky numbers, my lucky store, even a lucky pen to fill out the tickets."

The turning point came during a Sunday service when Pastor Martinez was preaching about the golden calf. "He said something that hit me like a lightning bolt: 'The Israelites didn't stop believing in God when they made the golden calf. They just created a god they could control when the real God felt absent.'"

Rachel realized she hadn't stopped believing in God. She'd just created a supplemental god—one that drew its power from her weekly offerings and promised to answer her prayers on a predictable schedule.

"I was still praying to God about my finances," she explains. "But I was trusting lottery tickets to actually do something about them. I had created this weird hybrid religion where God was good for spiritual stuff, but Powerball was better for practical stuff."

> **READER REFLECTION** *Take an honest inventory: What do you turn to when prayer feels too slow? When God's timing doesn't match your timeline? That thing—whether it's lottery tickets, get-rich-quick schemes, or something else—might be functioning as an idol in your life.*

The conviction was immediate. Rachel threw away $35 worth of tickets that night—tickets for drawings that hadn't happened yet.

"My kids thought I'd lost my mind," she laughs. "They kept asking, 'Mom, what if those were the winning numbers?' And I told them, 'Then God will find another way to provide.'"

He did. Within two months, Rachel was offered overtime shifts. Within six months, she'd received a promotion. Within a year, she'd started a side business doing medical consulting that now provides more income than her original job.

"Looking back," Rachel reflects, "every dollar I spent on lottery tickets was like putting money in the offering plate of a false church. I was literally funding my own idolatry."

The Biblical Pattern of Idol-Making

The Israelites' golden calf wasn't their first or last dance with idolatry. Throughout the Old Testament, we see a consistent pattern:

1. **God delays** (from their perspective)
2. **People panic**
3. **People create** an alternative god
4. **God responds** with both judgment and mercy
5. **People repent** (temporarily)
6. **The cycle repeats**

Sound familiar?

1. **God's provision seems delayed** (the bills are due, the situation is urgent)
2. **We panic** (anxiety replaces peace)
3. **We create** an alternative source of hope (lottery tickets, get-rich-quick schemes)
4. **God responds** with discipline designed to restore us
5. **We repent** ("I'll never buy another ticket")
6. **The cycle repeats** (until we address the root issue: our faith in God's provision)

The Smartphone Shrine

But lottery tickets aren't the only modern idols that fit in our pockets. Consider the smartphone—another small god that promises to meet needs only God can truly fulfill:

- **Connection** (what God offers through relationship with Him)
- **Knowledge** (what God provides through wisdom)
- **Entertainment** (what God gives through joy)
- **Validation** (what God supplies through His love)
- **Purpose** (what God grants through calling)

The average American checks their phone 96 times per day. That's once every 10 minutes during waking hours. If that's not devotional behavior, what is?

Like lottery tickets, smartphones become idols not because they're inherently evil, but because we ask them to provide what only God can give. We worship them not with our words but with our attention, our hope, and our time.

The Cryptocurrency Golden Calf

The newest golden calf on the block? Cryptocurrency.

"I'll admit it," says Marcus Rivera, a 34-year-old software engineer from Austin. "When Bitcoin was skyrocketing in 2021, I completely lost my mind. I was checking prices every five minutes, reading crypto Twitter instead of Scripture, and staying up until 3 AM watching charts."

Marcus had been a solid believer for fifteen years, but the promise of cryptocurrency wealth awakened something he didn't expect: idolatry.

"I stopped tithing because I needed every dollar to buy more crypto. I stopped my regular prayer time because I was too busy researching the next big coin. I was still going to church, but my heart was completely focused on my portfolio."

The crash of 2022 was Marcus's Mount Sinai moment. "I lost 80% of my investment in six months. But more importantly, I realized I'd lost my peace, my joy, and my trust in God. I'd replaced the Creator with creation—digital creation, but creation nonetheless."

Marcus liquidated his remaining crypto holdings and recommitted to tithing and regular spiritual disciplines. "I learned that it doesn't matter if your idol is made of gold, paper, or blockchain. If you're trusting it to provide what only God can provide, it's a golden calf."

> **LOTTERY FACT BOX** *Research shows that people who regularly play the lottery show decreased creative problem-solving abilities over time. When we repeatedly turn to chance-based solutions, we literally atrophy our innovative thinking muscles. The brain stops looking for solutions because it's been trained to wait for external rescue.*

Breaking the Idol Factory

The solution to modern idolatry isn't trying harder to avoid false gods. It's falling deeper in love with the true God.

When Moses came down from Mount Sinai and saw the golden calf, he didn't just destroy the idol. He climbed back up the mountain and spent another forty days in God's presence. The answer to false worship is true worship.

Here's how to identify and eliminate the golden calves in your life:

The 3:00 AM Test What do you think about when you can't sleep? What occupies your mind during anxiety attacks? Whatever you turn to for comfort when God feels distant—that's probably an idol.

The Wallet Test Look at your spending over the last three months. Where is your money going? What are you funding? Your treasure reveals your heart (Matthew 6:21).

The Time Test What gets your prime time? What do you check first in the morning and last at night? What consumes your thoughts during commutes or quiet moments?

The Hope Test Complete this sentence: "If I could just _____, everything would be okay." Whatever fills that blank is probably an idol.

The Crisis Test When crisis hits, what's your first instinct? Do you pray, or do you scheme? Do you seek God, or do you seek solutions that bypass God?

The God Who Doesn't Fit in Pockets

The beauty of the real God is that He can't be reduced to something we can carry around and control. He's too big for our pockets, too wise for our manipulation, too loving for our transaction-based approaches.

Isaiah 55:8-9 reminds us: "'For my thoughts are not your thoughts, neither are your ways my ways,' declares the Lord. 'As the heavens are higher than the earth, so are my ways higher than your ways and my thoughts than your thoughts.'"

This isn't a limitation of God—it's the liberation of worship. We don't have to manage God, control Him, or figure out how to make Him respond to our needs. We get to trust Him, rest in His wisdom, and watch Him work in ways that surpass our highest hopes.

PRACTICAL EXERCISE: The Idol Inventory

For the next week, carry a small notebook or use your phone to track every time you:

- Check lottery results or buy tickets
- Scroll social media when anxious
- Shop online to feel better
- Check your bank account obsessively
- Turn to anything other than prayer when stressed

At the end of the week, review your patterns. What does this reveal about your functional gods versus your stated beliefs?

The Great Exchange

God isn't asking you to give up your golden calves so you can have nothing. He's asking you to exchange your small gods for the big God, your manageable deities for the unmanageable Creator, your pocket-sized promises for universe-sized provision.

When you throw away your lottery tickets, you're not losing hope. You're trading false hope for real hope.

When you delete gambling apps from your phone, you're not limiting your options. You're expanding them to include divine possibilities you never considered.

When you stop trying to create gods you can control, you gain access to the God who controls everything—including the things you thought were random.

The Testimony of Empty Pockets

Six months after Rachel threw away her lottery tickets, she had a conversation with her eight-year-old daughter that changed both their lives.

"Mom," little Emma said, "you seem happier now that you stopped buying those tickets."

"Why do you think that is, baby?"

Emma thought for a moment. "Because now when you pray, you actually believe God is going to answer."

Out of the mouths of babes.

Rachel realized that her daughter had been watching her create and worship golden calves for years. But Emma had also watched her destroy them and return to the real God.

"Now when we pray together," Rachel says, "there's no competition. It's not God vs. the lottery for our trust. It's just God. And that makes all the difference."

> **YOUR MIRROR QUESTION** *If God provided everything you needed without you ever winning the lottery, buying the right cryptocurrency, finding the perfect investment, or catching the lucky break you're hoping for—would that be enough? If the answer is anything other than an immediate "yes," you've identified your idol.*

The Question That Destroys Idols

Before we move to the next chapter, let me ask you the same question that destroyed my own paper idols:

If God provided everything you needed without you ever winning the lottery, buying the right cryptocurrency, finding the perfect investment, or catching the lucky break you're hoping for—would that be enough?

If the answer is anything other than an immediate "yes," you've identified your idol.

The good news? Idols are designed to be destroyed. They're made by human hands to meet human needs, but they're no match for the God who made the hands, the needs, and the humans themselves.

Your pocket doesn't need golden calves. It needs the name of the One who owns the cattle on a thousand hills, the wealth in every mine, and the solution to every problem you'll ever face.

That God doesn't fit in your pocket.

He fills the universe.

And He's been waiting patiently for you to stop worshiping what fits in your hand and start trusting what holds your life.

Next up: Chapter 4, *where we'll explore the cosmic awkwardness of trying to hide our lottery habits from an omniscient God, and why He's not impressed with our lucky numbers.*

CHAPTER 4

God Knows Your Powerball Numbers (And He's Not Impressed)

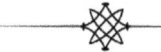

"Nothing in all creation is hidden from God's sight. Everything is uncovered and laid bare before the eyes of him to whom we must give account." ---Hebrews 4:13

Maybe you're not a ministry leader, but you're the night-shift nurse who buys scratch-offs during your 3 AM break, carefully timing your purchases when the hospital corridors are empty and no one from your small group might see you.

Maybe you're not a pastor, but you're the accountant who has developed an elaborate system of cash withdrawals and gas station rotations to keep your lottery habit invisible to your spouse who thinks you've been using that money for lunch.

Maybe you've never preached about God's omniscience, but you've found yourself praying in the car after buying tickets, somehow hoping that if you ask God to bless your numbers, it makes the whole thing spiritual rather than shameful.

If any of this sounds familiar, then you know the exhausting mental gymnastics of trying to hide something from Someone who sees everything.

LOTTERY FACT BOX *According to financial behavior researchers, people who regularly gamble spend an average of 23% more mental energy on financial deception and cover-up strategies than non-gamblers. This cognitive load actually impairs decision-making in other areas of life, creating a cycle where poor choices compound over time.*

I used to think I was being sneaky.

The gas station visits at odd hours. The cash transactions that wouldn't show up on credit card statements. The tickets tucked behind other papers in my wallet. The careful timing—buying tickets when my wife was at work, checking numbers when she was in the shower.

I thought I had developed a foolproof system for keeping my lottery habit private. I'd covered all the bases, managed all the variables, accounted for every contingency.

There was just one problem with my master plan: I forgot about God.

Not intellectually, of course. I knew God was omniscient. I'd preached sermons about God seeing all, knowing all, being present everywhere. But somehow, in the mental compartment where I justified my lottery purchases, I'd created a God-free zone. A cosmic blind spot where my actions couldn't be observed or judged.

Turns out, God doesn't have blind spots.

The Omniscience Problem

Psalm 139 is one of the most beautiful and terrifying passages in Scripture. David writes, "You have searched me, Lord, and you know me. You know when I sit and when I rise; you perceive my thoughts from afar. You discern my going out and my lying down; you are familiar with all my ways."

It's beautiful because it speaks to God's intimate knowledge of us. It's terrifying because it speaks to God's intimate knowledge of us.

There's no hiding from omniscience. No secret compartments in an all-seeing mind. No private moments with an ever-present God.

When I bought those lottery tickets, God was there. When I chose my numbers, He watched. When I hid them in my wallet, He saw. When I checked the results with racing heart and sweaty palms, He knew the numbers before they were drawn.

But here's what took me years to understand: God's omniscience isn't a surveillance system designed to catch us doing wrong. It's a love language designed to remind us that we're never alone.

Even when we're disappointing Him.

> **KINGDOM PRINCIPLE** *God's omniscience isn't divine espionage—it's divine intimacy. He knows everything about us not to condemn us, but to love us completely. Perfect knowledge enables perfect love, not perfect judgment.*

The Cosmic Awkwardness

Imagine trying to explain your lottery strategy to God.

"Well, Lord, I know You said You'd provide for all my needs, but I thought maybe You could use some help. I picked these numbers based on my kids' birthdays, which seems spiritual, right? And I've been praying over the tickets, which basically makes this a prayer request with better odds."

It sounds ridiculous when you put it that way, doesn't it?

But that's essentially what we're doing every time we buy a ticket while claiming to trust God's provision. We're presenting our heavenly Father with a backup plan to His sovereignty, an insurance policy against His faithfulness, a hedge bet against His promises.

The cosmic awkwardness isn't that God doesn't know what we're doing. It's that He knows exactly what we're doing, and He knows exactly why we're doing it.

What God Sees When We Play the Lottery

Let me paint you a picture of what our lottery habits look like from heaven's perspective:

God sees a child He loves desperately, a child He's promised to provide for, a child He's given talents and abilities and opportunities to flourish. But that child doesn't trust the promises, doesn't believe in the provision, doesn't have confidence in the plan.

So the child starts looking for alternatives. Better plans. Faster solutions. Easier paths.

God watches as His beloved child takes hard-earned money—money He provided through jobs He opened, skills He granted, opportunities He created—and hands it over to a system specifically designed to take advantage of mathematical ignorance and prey on financial desperation.

He sees His child praying for financial breakthrough while simultaneously funding an industry that profits from financial destruction.

He watches His child asking for His blessing on a venture that explicitly excludes Him from the equation.

God sees all of this, and His response isn't anger.

It's heartbreak.

> **CULTURAL SPOTLIGHT: The Psychology of Financial Secrecy** Dr. Brad Klontz, a financial psychologist, has found that financial secrecy within marriages increases the likelihood of financial infidelity by 400%. More striking: people who hide gambling habits from spouses are 3x more likely to develop other deceptive behaviors, creating what he calls "integrity erosion syndrome." The need to hide lottery tickets often leads to hiding other financial decisions, creating a cascade of trust issues.

The Difference Between Anger and Heartbreak

When my daughter was seven, she went through a phase where she was convinced that I didn't really love her. No matter what I said or did, she was sure I was just pretending, that eventually I'd get tired of her and leave.

During this phase, she started hoarding food in her bedroom. Crackers under her pillow. Fruit snacks in her dresser. Granola bars in her backpack. Not because she was hungry—we had plenty of food—but because she didn't trust that we'd keep feeding her.

When I discovered her stash, I wasn't angry. I was heartbroken. Not because she'd taken food, but because she felt like she needed to. Not because she'd hidden it from me, but because she didn't believe I'd take care of her.

That's how God feels when He watches us buy lottery tickets.

He's not angry that we spent two dollars. He's heartbroken that we felt like we needed to.

The Prayer God Never Answers

Have you ever prayed for God to help you win the lottery?

Be honest. If you've ever bought a ticket, you've probably prayed about it. Maybe not a formal, hands-folded, eyes-closed prayer, but some version of "God, if You want me to win this, let this be the one."

Here's why God never answers that prayer: He loves you too much.

Think about it. If God helped you win the lottery, what would that teach you about where provision comes from? What would it say about the reliability of His promises versus the reliability of random chance? How would it affect your faith the next time you faced a financial challenge?

God doesn't answer prayers that would ultimately destroy your trust in Him, even when you're convinced they would help you.

> **READER REFLECTION** Think about the prayers you've prayed regarding money, success, or security. How many of those prayers were asking God to change your circumstances versus asking God to change your character? What does this reveal about what you actually trust for provision?

Dr. Lisa Feldman Barrett, a neuroscientist at Northeastern University, has studied what she calls "reward system hijacking"—when artificial rewards replace natural ones, making the natural ones less satisfying over time.

"If you won the lottery after praying about it," Dr. Barrett explains, "your brain would create a neurological pathway linking prayer to gambling rather than prayer to relationship with God. You'd essentially be training your brain to see God as a cosmic slot machine rather than a loving Father."

God's refusal to help us win the lottery isn't divine stinginess. It's divine protection.

The Omniscient God Who Pretends Not to Know

But here's where God's response gets really beautiful: Sometimes He acts like He doesn't know.

Not because He doesn't actually know, but because love sometimes means giving people the dignity of confession rather than the humiliation of exposure.

When Adam and Eve hid in the Garden after eating the forbidden fruit, God called out, "Where are you?" (Genesis 3:9). Not because He didn't know where they were, but because He wanted to give them the opportunity to come out of hiding voluntarily.

When Cain killed Abel, God asked, "Where is your brother Abel?" (Genesis 4:9). Not because He didn't know what had happened, but because He wanted to give Cain a chance to tell the truth.

God knows about your lottery tickets. He knows about your scratch-offs. He knows about your online gambling, your casino visits, your sports betting apps. He knows about every backup plan you've created to His provision.

But He's waiting for you to tell Him about it.

Not because He needs the information, but because you need the confession.

The Story of Tom Williams

Tom Williams is a pastor in Oklahoma who learned this lesson the hard way.

For three years, Tom had been struggling to keep his small church afloat. Attendance was declining, giving was down, and he was working two part-time jobs just to make ends meet personally. The stress was affecting his marriage, his health, and his ministry.

"I started buying lottery tickets as what I called 'financial prayer,'" Tom admits. "I figured if God wanted to provide for the church through a lottery win, who was I to limit His methods?"

Tom had elaborate theological justifications for his habit. He calculated exactly how much he'd give to the church if he won. He researched which ministries he'd support. He even preached a sermon series on "God's Unexpected Provision" that was really just a way to justify his lottery theology.

But the breakthrough came during a men's retreat when Tom was leading a session on honesty in prayer.

"I was teaching about bringing our real struggles to God, not hiding anything from Him, being completely transparent in our prayer life," Tom recalls. "And right in the middle of talking about honesty with God, I realized I'd been lying to Him for three years."

Not lying with words, but lying with actions. Every lottery ticket was a declaration that God's promises weren't sufficient. Every drawing was a vote of no confidence in divine provision.

"That night, I confessed everything to God," Tom says. "Not because He didn't know, but because I needed Him to know that I knew He knew."

The relief was immediate. "It was like I'd been holding my breath for three years and finally exhaled."

PRACTICAL EXERCISE: The Honesty Audit

For the next 24 hours, practice radical honesty with God about your financial fears and lottery thoughts:

1. **Morning**: Tell God exactly what you're worried about financially today
2. **Midday**: Confess any moments when you've trusted chance more than His character
3. **Evening**: Thank Him for one way He's already provided that you might have overlooked
4. **Before bed**: Ask Him to reveal any areas where you're trying to hide from His omniscience

Notice how confession creates relief rather than condemnation.

The Mathematics of Omniscience

Here's a sobering thought: God knows the outcome of every lottery drawing before it happens.

He knows which numbers will be drawn on Saturday. He knows your numbers won't match. He knows you're going to be disappointed again. He knows you're going to buy more tickets next week.

And He watches anyway.

Not because He enjoys watching you lose, but because He's hoping you'll eventually realize that the game itself is rigged—not just mathematically, but spiritually.

The lottery industry makes $31 billion in profit annually. That's $31 billion extracted from people who are hoping to win but statistically guaranteed to lose. God sees that extraction as a form of oppression—the financially desperate being exploited by the financially sophisticated.

When you buy lottery tickets, you're not just gambling with your money. You're participating in a system that God sees as predatory toward the very people He's called His children to protect.

The Surveillance vs. The Shepherd

There's a difference between God knowing everything as a surveillance state and God knowing everything as a loving shepherd.

In a surveillance state, information is gathered to control and punish. With a loving shepherd, information is gathered to protect and provide.

God's omniscience isn't Big Brother watching to catch you doing wrong. It's a Good Shepherd watching to keep you from harm.

When God sees you buying lottery tickets, He's not taking notes for a future punishment. He's grieving that His child is settling for so much less than what He has planned.

Imagine a millionaire father watching his son dig through trash cans looking for food. The father isn't angry that his son is hungry. He's heartbroken that his son doesn't believe the family fortune is available to him.

That's God watching us play the lottery.

> **LOTTERY FACT BOX** *Studies show that people who regularly play the lottery experience a 34% decrease in their ability to recognize genuine opportunities for financial improvement. The brain becomes so focused on random chance that it literally stops noticing skill-based or relationship-based opportunities for advancement.*

The Story of Mike's Casino Security

My friend Mike learned about God's omniscience in the most unexpected place: a casino security room.

Mike worked for years as a security coordinator at a major casino in Las Vegas. His job was to watch the surveillance cameras and look for cheaters, thieves, and problem gamblers.

"I spent eight hours a day watching people make decisions they thought were private," Mike says. "I saw the businessman who told his wife he was in meetings while he was actually losing the mortgage payment at blackjack. I saw the grandmother who said she was shopping but was really feeding her Social Security check into slot machines."

What struck Mike wasn't the gambling itself, but the elaborate deceptions people created to hide their gambling.

"They'd park their cars in different sections of the garage so spouses wouldn't see them. They'd use cash advances to hide transactions. They'd create fictional meetings and appointments to justify their time away. The mental energy they spent covering their tracks was exhausting to watch."

Mike's perspective on surveillance changed his understanding of God's omniscience. "I realized that God's all-seeing eye isn't like a casino's security system. Casinos watch to catch and punish. God watches to love and restore."

Mike eventually left the casino industry and is now a counselor specializing in gambling addiction. "I tell my clients, 'God already knows about your habit. The question isn't whether you can hide it from Him. The question is whether you'll let Him help you with it.'"

The Freedom of Being Known

There's something liberating about realizing you can't hide from God.

It means you can stop trying.

You can stop the elaborate cover-ups, the careful timing, the strategic misdirection. You can stop pretending your lottery habit is occasional entertainment when it's really become a regular payment to false hope.

You can stop acting like your gambling is a private matter when it's affecting your relationship with the God who promises to provide for all your needs.

When you realize God already knows everything, confession becomes relief rather than revelation.

The Prayer That Changes Everything

The most powerful prayer I've ever prayed about my lottery habit wasn't a request. It was an acknowledgment:

"God, You know I've been buying lottery tickets. You know I've been trusting them more than I've been trusting You. You know I've been hoping they would provide what You've already promised to provide. I'm not telling You anything You don't know, but I need You to know that I know You know."

That prayer didn't change God's knowledge of my situation. It changed my relationship with His knowledge.

Instead of God's omniscience being something to hide from, it became something to run to.

The God Who Numbers Your Tickets

Psalm 139:4 says, "Before a word is on my tongue you, Lord, know it completely."

If God knows our words before we speak them, He certainly knows our numbers before we pick them.

He knows that 7-14-21-35-42-8 won't win on Saturday. He knows that Quick Pick isn't actually quick luck. He knows that your "lucky" numbers have never been lucky.

But He also knows something else: He knows exactly what you're looking for when you buy those tickets, and He knows exactly how to provide it without requiring you to beat 292-million-to-1 odds.

The question isn't whether God knows your numbers.

The question is whether you're ready to trust His.

The Divine Alternative

God has better numbers than your Powerball picks:

Matthew 6:33 - "Seek first his kingdom and his righteousness, and all these things will be given to you as well."

Philippians 4:19 - "And my God will meet all your needs according to the riches of his glory in Christ Jesus."

2 Corinthians 9:8 - "God is able to bless you abundantly, so that in all things at all times, having all that you need, you will abound in every good work."

Jeremiah 29:11 - "'For I know the plans I have for you,' declares the Lord, 'plans to prosper you and not to harm you, to give you hope and a future.'"

These aren't lottery numbers you have to match. They're promises you get to claim.

> **YOUR MIRROR QUESTION** *What would change in your life if you truly believed that God's complete knowledge of you leads to His complete love for you, not His complete judgment of you? How would knowing that He sees everything affect your trust in His provision?*

The Moment of Truth

So here's your moment of truth: Will you keep pretending God doesn't see your lottery tickets, or will you start trusting that He sees everything—including solutions you haven't considered, provisions you haven't imagined, and blessings you haven't dreamed of?

God knows your Powerball numbers. He's not impressed.

But He's deeply impressed by faith that doesn't need backup plans. He's moved by trust that doesn't require guarantees. He's honored by prayers that don't hedge their bets.

Your omniscient God isn't watching to catch you in the act of buying lottery tickets. He's watching to catch you in the act of trusting Him completely.

And He's been waiting patiently for you to give Him that chance.

Next up: Chapter 5, where we'll discover what Jesus really meant by "abundant life" and why it has nothing to do with matching six numbers.

CHAPTER 5

The Abundant Life That Doesn't Need Six Matching Numbers

"I have come that they may have life, and have it to the full." --- John 10:10

Maybe you're not a healthcare worker, but you're the retail manager who dreams about what "the good life" would look like—no more demanding customers, no more tight budgets, no more stress about your kids' college funds—if you could just hit those six numbers.

Maybe you're not a nurse, but you're the single parent who lies awake calculating how lottery winnings could solve everything: the mortgage, the car repairs, the medical bills, the overwhelming feeling that you're always one emergency away from disaster.

Maybe you've never cared for hospital patients, but you've witnessed your own version of the ultimate irony: people who have everything money can buy but still seem desperately unhappy, while others who have very little somehow radiate contentment and joy.

The Abundant Life That Doesn't Need Six Matching Numbers

If you've ever wondered why wealth doesn't guarantee happiness—or why the lottery promises abundance but rarely delivers satisfaction—then you're ready to discover what Jesus actually meant when He promised "abundant life."

LOTTERY FACT BOX *A Princeton University study tracking lottery winners over 20 years found that 89% reported their life satisfaction returning to pre-win levels within 18 months. More striking: 44% said they were less happy five years after winning than they had been before. The study concluded that sudden wealth without character development typically creates more problems than it solves.*

The first time I heard about William "Bud" Post III, I was sitting in a hospital break room during my nursing shift, reading a magazine article that would change how I thought about winning forever.

Bud had won $16.2 million in the Pennsylvania lottery in 1988. By 1993, he was $1 million in debt. His brother had hired a hitman to kill him. His landlady had successfully sued him for a third of his winnings. He'd been arrested for firing a shotgun at a bill collector. He'd lost houses, cars, businesses, and most of his family relationships.

"I wish it never happened," Bud told reporters before his death in 2006. "It was totally a nightmare."

As I sat there in my scrubs, having just finished a twelve-hour shift caring for people fighting for their lives, I was struck by the cosmic irony: Here was a man who'd won what millions consider the ultimate prize, and he called it a nightmare. Meanwhile, I'd just spent my day with patients who had nothing but somehow radiated more peace, joy, and contentment than a lottery millionaire.

That's when it hit me: We've got the definition of abundant life completely backwards.

The Abundance Industry

Somewhere along the way, we started believing that abundant life meant abundance of stuff. The American dream got confused with the abundant life Jesus promised, and we began measuring blessing by the size of our bank accounts rather than the depth of our peace.

The lottery industry feeds on this confusion. Their marketing doesn't really sell tickets—it sells a vision of the abundant life. Look at any lottery commercial and you'll see the same themes:

- Freedom from financial worry
- Time to spend with family
- Ability to help others
- Security for the future
- Joy and fulfillment

These aren't evil desires. They're human longings that echo the abundant life Jesus actually promised. The problem isn't wanting these things—it's looking for them in random numbers instead of relationship with God.

> **KINGDOM PRINCIPLE** *True abundance isn't about having more things—it's about needing fewer things to be satisfied. The abundant life Jesus promised grows from internal contentment, not external accumulation.*

What Jesus Actually Meant

When Jesus said, "I have come that they may have life, and have it to the full" (John 10:10), He wasn't talking about full bank accounts. He was talking about full hearts.

The context of this verse is crucial. Jesus is describing Himself as the Good Shepherd who provides everything His sheep need. He's contrasting His care with thieves who "come only to steal and kill and destroy."

In other words, Jesus is saying: "I'm here to give you a life so rich, so full, so satisfying that you'll never need to look to thieves and destroyers for what you think you're missing."

The lottery is a thief. It steals hope by misdirecting it. It kills contentment by promising that happiness is just one drawing away. It destroys the very faith that could provide the abundant life it pretends to offer.

The Abundant Life Paradox

Here's what I've learned after four decades in healthcare: The people with the most abundant lives often have the least abundant possessions.

I've cared for millionaires who were miserable and minimum-wage workers who were genuinely joyful. I've seen cancer patients who radiated peace and healthy people consumed by anxiety. I've known lottery winners who felt empty and church janitors who felt rich.

The abundant life isn't about having more. It's about needing less.

> **CULTURAL SPOTLIGHT: The Lottery Winner's Curse** Jack Whittaker won $314 million in 2002—then the largest jackpot in U.S. history. Within five years, his granddaughter had died of a drug overdose, his daughter died under mysterious circumstances, his wife left him, and his businesses failed. "I wish I'd torn that ticket up," he later said. Psychologists have documented that roughly 70% of lottery winners lose or spend all their winnings within five years, and studies show lottery winners are no happier than non-winners within 18 months.

The Story of Mrs. Rodriguez

Let me tell you about Elena Rodriguez, a patient I cared for during my psychiatric nursing years. Elena was a 67-year-old grandmother who'd come to us after a severe depression following her husband's death. She'd lost her home to medical bills, was living in a tiny apartment, and surviving on Social Security.

By every worldly measure, Elena had nothing. But over the weeks I cared for her, I watched something remarkable happen. As she processed her grief and reconnected with her faith, Elena began to discover what she called "the riches I'd forgotten I had."

"I have five grandchildren who love me," she told me one day. "I have hands that can still cook their favorite meals. I have a voice that can still sing their favorite songs. I have stories that can still make them laugh. I have prayers that still reach heaven."

Elena's depression lifted not because her circumstances changed, but because her definition of abundance changed. She stopped measuring her wealth by what she'd lost and started measuring it by what could never be taken away.

Six months after her discharge, Elena sent me a card. "I used to buy lottery tickets every week," she wrote, "hoping to win enough money to feel rich. Now I know I was already rich. I just needed new eyes to see it."

The Matthew 6:33 Experiment

"But seek first his kingdom and his righteousness, and all these things will be given to you as well" (Matthew 6:33).

This verse isn't a formula for getting rich. It's a recipe for abundant living. When we seek God's kingdom first, we discover something revolutionary: We already have everything we need for a rich, full, satisfying life.

I decided to test this principle when I was struggling with my own lottery temptations. Instead of buying tickets, I committed to investing that money in kingdom activities for 90 days:

- $20 went to supporting a missionary family
- $15 bought groceries for a struggling church member
- $10 funded a scholarship for a nursing student

- $25 supported our church's community outreach

The result? I experienced more joy, peace, and sense of purpose than any lottery jackpot could have provided. I was participating in God's abundant life by becoming a channel of His abundance to others.

> **READER REFLECTION** *Take a moment to list everything you have that money can't buy: relationships, memories, skills, experiences, faith, health, opportunities. Now list what you think you need money to obtain. Compare the two lists. Which contains the things that actually make life meaningful?*

The Creativity Connection

Remember, you were made in the image of God, and the first thing we learn about God is that He's creative (Genesis 1:1). This means the abundant life includes discovering and expressing your creative capacity.

The lottery promises to give you money you didn't earn for problems you haven't solved. God promises to give you ideas you haven't considered for problems you're uniquely equipped to address.

Take Sarah Chen, a nurse I met at a conference. Sarah had been buying lottery tickets for years, dreaming of winning enough money to start a nonprofit serving elderly patients. During our conversation, I asked, "What if instead of hoping to win money to start your nonprofit, you started your nonprofit and trusted God to fund it?"

"I can't start a nonprofit without money," she protested.

"What could you start without money?" I asked.

That question changed everything. Sarah began by volunteering at nursing homes on her days off. She started a social media page sharing elderly care tips. She organized other nurses to volunteer with her. Within eighteen months, her volunteer organization had become a recognized nonprofit with grant funding and corporate sponsors.

"I wasted five years hoping to win money to start helping people," Sarah reflects, "when I could have been helping people and trusting God to provide the money."

The Abundance Audit

If you want to discover the abundant life Jesus offers, try conducting an "abundance audit" of your current situation:

Relational Abundance:
- Who loves you?
- Who can you call at 2 AM?
- Who makes you laugh?
- Who trusts you with their struggles?

Creative Abundance:
- What can you build, make, or create?

- What problems can you solve?
- What skills do you possess?
- What ideas have you never pursued?

Spiritual Abundance:

- How has God been faithful to you?
- What prayers has He answered?
- What character has He developed in you?
- How have you grown through challenges?

Physical Abundance:

- What does your body enable you to do?
- What beauty can you appreciate?
- What experiences can you enjoy?
- What adventures are still possible?

Most people who complete this audit realize they're already living an abundant life—they just hadn't been measuring it correctly.

PRACTICAL EXERCISE: The 30-Day Abundance Challenge

For the next 30 days, instead of hoping to win the lottery, practice winning at life:

1. **Morning gratitude:** Before checking your phone, list three things you're grateful for

2. **Daily creativity:** Use your God-given gifts to create something, solve something, or help someone
3. **Evening reflection:** Before bed, identify one way you experienced God's abundance that day
4. **Weekly giving:** Give generously of your time, talents, or treasure, trusting God to replenish what you share
5. **Monthly service:** Find a way to serve others, discovering that blessing others creates abundance in your own life

The Suburban Millionaire

I once knew a man who lived in the suburbs of New York—let's call him David—who made $300,000 a year but felt desperately poor. He lived in a beautiful home, drove luxury cars, and took expensive vacations, but he was constantly anxious about money, constantly comparing himself to others, constantly looking for ways to make more.

David bought lottery tickets religiously, convinced that a big win would finally give him the security and happiness he was seeking.

Then David lost his job during a corporate downsizing. For six months, his family lived on unemployment benefits and savings. They canceled the vacations, sold one car, ate dinner at home every night.

"Those six months were the happiest our family had been in years," David told me later. "We played board games instead of watching TV. We took walks instead of going shopping. We talked to each other instead of being distracted by our phones. We discovered that we already had everything we needed for a rich life—we'd just been too busy acquiring stuff to notice."

David eventually found another job, but at half his previous salary. "We could go back to our old lifestyle," he said, "but why would we? We've discovered what abundant life actually feels like."

The Widow's Abundance

The Bible's clearest picture of abundant life might be found in the poorest person in Scripture: the widow who gave two small coins to the temple treasury (Mark 12:41-44).

Jesus watched wealthy people give large amounts, but He was moved by the widow who "out of her poverty, put in everything—all she had to live on."

This woman had no savings account, no retirement plan, no lottery tickets, no backup strategy. She had nothing but trust in God's provision. And Jesus held her up as the example of abundant living.

The abundant life isn't about having enough money to be independent of God. It's about trusting God so completely that you don't need independence from Him.

> **LOTTERY FACT BOX** Dr. Sarah Stanley Fallaw, who studies wealthy individuals, has found that people who build wealth through what she calls "providence and provision" (gradual, character-based wealth building) maintain their wealth at rates exceeding 90%. Meanwhile, lottery winners lose their wealth at rates exceeding 70%. There's a fundamental difference between wealth that comes with wisdom and wealth that comes without it.

The Peace Dividend

Beyond material benefits, the abundant life provides what economists might call a "peace dividend"—the immeasurable value of rest, contentment, and freedom from anxiety.

Philippians 4:19 doesn't just promise provision; it promises peace: "And my God will meet all your needs according to the riches of his glory in Christ Jesus." This verse comes in the context of Paul's teaching about contentment and freedom from worry.

Lottery winners frequently report increased anxiety after winning. They worry about losing their money, about people taking advantage of them, about making wrong decisions with their windfall. The abundant life brings the opposite experience—decreased anxiety and increased peace.

I've observed this phenomenon countless times in healthcare settings. Patients who trusted in God's abundant provision faced medical crises with remarkable peace, while those who trusted in luck or chance often experienced paralyzing anxiety even during minor health issues.

The Practice of Abundance

If you want to experience abundant life, stop practicing scarcity. Here's how:

Instead of: "I can't afford to give."
Practice: "I can't afford not to give."

Instead of: "I need more to be happy."
Practice: "I have enough to be grateful."

Instead of: "If only I could win the lottery."
Practice: "What if I already have everything I need?"

Instead of: "God isn't providing fast enough."
Practice: "God's timing is perfect."

The Ultimate Lottery

Here's the ultimate irony: You've already won the only lottery that matters.

The odds of you being born at all were approximately 400 trillion to 1. The odds of you being born in a time and place where you have access to the Gospel, education, healthcare, and opportunities? Incalculable.

You won the genetic lottery by being made in God's image. You won the spiritual lottery by being offered salvation through Christ. You won the creative lottery by being given unique gifts and abilities. You won the relational lottery by being loved by the Creator of the universe.

The abundant life isn't about winning more. It's about recognizing what you've already won.

When Enough Becomes Enough

The secret to abundant life is reaching the place where enough is enough. Not because you've stopped wanting growth or improvement, but because you've stopped believing that your worth, joy, peace, or purpose depends on acquiring more.

Paul knew this secret: "I have learned to be content whatever the circumstances" (Philippians 4:11). His contentment wasn't based on his situation but on his relationship with the God who promised to meet all his needs.

Contentment isn't settling for less. It's recognizing that you already have more than you realized.

> **YOUR MIRROR QUESTION** *If you discovered today that you would never be wealthy by conventional standards, but you could have deep relationships, meaningful work, perfect health, and unshakeable peace—would that be enough? What does your answer reveal about what you really believe about abundant life?*

The Life That's Actually Full

The abundant life Jesus promised isn't waiting for you to win it in some future drawing. It's available right now, in your current circumstances, with your present resources, through your existing relationships.

You don't need six matching numbers. You need one matching heart—a heart that matches God's heart, trusts His provision, and finds its satisfaction in His presence rather than His presents.

The lottery promises abundance after you win. Jesus promises abundance while you wait.

The lottery offers abundance through chance. Jesus offers abundance through choice.

The lottery provides abundance to the lucky few. Jesus provides abundance to the faithful many.

Stop playing the lottery of chance. Start living the abundant life of faith.

You've already won everything that matters. It's time to start collecting your prize.

Next up: Chapter 6, where we'll discover what "seek first the kingdom" actually means in practical, everyday terms, and why it's the ultimate alternative to lottery thinking.

CHAPTER 6

Seek First the Kingdom (The Rest is Just Details)

"But seek first his kingdom and his righteousness, and all these things will be given to you as well." ---Matthew 6:33

Maybe you're not a psychiatric nurse, but you're the office manager who finds yourself at 3 AM mentally calculating bills, wondering how you'll cover everything this month, whispering the same desperate prayer: "God, if You could just help me win something—anything—everything would be okay."

Maybe you're not a healthcare worker, but you're the small business owner who's been faithful to God for years, tithing when you could barely afford it, serving at church despite exhaustion, yet still struggling financially while watching others seem to prosper effortlessly.

Maybe you've never worked in a hospital, but you've had your own version of standing in a supply closet at 3 AM, counting resources while the noise of crisis echoes nearby, wondering why seeking God doesn't seem to solve your most pressing problems.

If you've ever felt like you're doing everything right spiritually but still losing financially, then you're ready to discover what "seek first the kingdom" actually means—and why it's the ultimate solution to lottery thinking.

> **LOTTERY FACT BOX** *Research by behavioral economists shows that people who regularly buy lottery tickets spend 67% less time developing practical financial skills than non-players. The mental energy devoted to hoping for random rescue actually reduces investment in the skills that create real financial improvement. In other words, lottery thinking doesn't just waste money—it wastes the motivation to build wealth.*

The first time I really understood Matthew 6:33, I was standing in the supply closet of a psychiatric unit at 3 AM, counting medication while a patient down the hall was having a meltdown about money.

Mr. Johnson—not his real name—had been admitted after a suicide attempt triggered by gambling debts. For two hours, he'd been pacing his room, muttering the same phrase over and over: "If I could just win once. Just once. Everything would be okay."

As I listened to his anguish through the thin walls, I realized we were saying the same thing, just in different ways. He was saying, "If I could just win the lottery, everything would be okay." I was thinking, "If God would just provide financially, everything would be okay."

Both of us had it backwards.

We were seeking first our circumstances, hoping the kingdom would follow. But Jesus said it the other way around: Seek first the kingdom, and everything else gets added to you.

Standing in that supply closet, surrounded by medications designed to treat symptoms while patients struggled with deeper issues, I finally understood: Matthew 6:33 isn't a promise about God giving us more stuff. It's a promise about God making us the kind of people who don't need more stuff to be okay.

> **KINGDOM PRINCIPLE** *Seeking first the kingdom doesn't mean God becomes your financial advisor—it means you become His kingdom representative. When your primary focus shifts from getting provision to being provision for others, everything changes.*

The Upside-Down Kingdom

Jesus had a way of flipping conventional wisdom on its head, and Matthew 6:33 might be His most radical reversal of all.

The world says: Get your finances right, then you can focus on spiritual things.

Jesus says: Get your spiritual priorities right, and I'll handle your finances.

The world says: Secure your future first, then you can be generous.

Jesus says: Be generous first, and I'll secure your future.

The world says: Make sure you have enough, then trust God with the rest.

Jesus says: Trust God with everything, and you'll discover you already have enough.

This isn't just nice theology—it's practical economics. But it only works when we understand what "seeking first the kingdom" actually means.

What It Means to Seek the Kingdom

After decades of hearing sermons on Matthew 6:33, I used to think seeking the kingdom meant praying more, reading my Bible more, going to church more. Those things matter, but they're not the kingdom—they're tools for discovering the kingdom.

The kingdom of heaven isn't a place you go; it's a way you live. It's what happens when God's will is done "on earth as it is in heaven" (Matthew 6:10). It's when God's values become your values, God's priorities become your priorities, and God's methods become your methods.

Here's what seeking first the kingdom looks like in practical terms:

1. Seeking God's Solution Instead of Your Own

When faced with financial pressure, our natural instinct is to look for financial solutions: work more hours, find a second job, cut expenses, or—if desperation sets in—buy lottery tickets.

Seeking first the kingdom means asking different questions:

- "God, what are you trying to teach me through this situation?"
- "How can I grow in character while I wait for provision?"
- "What creative solutions haven't I considered?"
- "Who can I serve while I'm struggling?"

2. Seeking God's Timing Instead of Your Timeline

The lottery appeals to our desire for instant solutions. Buy a ticket Tuesday, change your life by Thursday. Seeking the kingdom means trusting God's timeline even when it's longer than we'd prefer.

3. Seeking God's Methods Instead of the World's Shortcuts

The world offers shortcuts to everything: instant wealth, instant success, instant happiness. The kingdom operates differently. God's methods usually involve:

- Character development through challenges
- Gradual growth rather than sudden transformation
- Community support rather than individual achievement

- Generosity rather than accumulation

> **CULTURAL SPOTLIGHT: The Instant Gratification Economy** *Americans now expect 2-day delivery as standard, 2-hour delivery as premium, and 2-minute download times as acceptable. This "instant everything" culture makes lottery tickets feel normal—just another form of instant gratification. But researchers have found that people who can delay gratification for meaningful goals are 42% more likely to achieve financial independence than those who seek immediate rewards.*

The Johnson Experiment

Let me tell you how Mr. Johnson learned to seek first the kingdom, and how it changed everything.

After his initial crisis, Mr. Johnson spent three weeks in our care. During that time, he participated in financial counseling, addiction recovery groups, and something we called "kingdom economics" sessions—discussions about finding security in God rather than gambling.

The breakthrough came when Mr. Johnson stopped asking, "How can I win money?" and started asking, "How can I serve people?"

Before his gambling addiction, Mr. Johnson had been a gifted mechanic. During his recovery, he began volunteering at a local ministry that provided car repairs for single mothers and elderly residents. He started with oil changes and basic maintenance, working for free while rebuilding his sense of purpose and self-worth.

"I spent five years trying to get rich by gambling," Mr. Johnson told me during a follow-up visit six months later. "I lost my house, my marriage, and almost my life. But in six months of seeking God's kingdom first—helping people instead of helping myself—I've gained more peace and purpose than I ever had when I was winning."

Mr. Johnson eventually started his own auto repair business with a sliding scale fee structure for low-income customers. His business thrived because he wasn't seeking first profit—he was seeking first service. The profit followed naturally.

"I used to think the kingdom was something you go to when you die," he reflected. "Now I know it's something you live in while you're alive. And it's a lot more rewarding than any jackpot."

> **READER REFLECTION** *Think about your current biggest worry or challenge. Now reframe it: Instead of asking "How can this problem be solved?" ask "How can serving others through this challenge help me grow and impact the kingdom?" Notice how the question changes your perspective and potential solutions.*

The 90-Day Kingdom Experiment

Inspired by stories like Mr. Johnson's, I decided to conduct my own experiment with Matthew 6:33. Instead of buying lottery tickets or scheming for financial advancement, I committed to seeking first the kingdom for 90 days. Here's what that looked like:

Days 1-30: Seeking God's Heart Instead of focusing on my financial needs, I focused on understanding God's character. I studied Scripture not for what God could do for me, but for who God is. I discovered that the God who "owns the cattle on a thousand hills" (Psalm 50:10) wasn't struggling to figure out how to meet my needs. My job wasn't to solve the provision problem—it was to trust the Provider.

Days 31-60: Seeking God's Purposes I shifted from asking "How can my needs be met?" to "How can I meet others' needs?" I volunteered at our church's food bank. I tutored struggling nursing students. I used my musical skills to play piano at nursing homes. Suddenly, my own financial worries seemed smaller in the context of serving others' larger needs.

Days 61-90: Seeking God's Ways I began looking for creative solutions to financial challenges instead of hoping for magical solutions. I refinanced my car at a lower rate. I negotiated better terms on our insurance. I started a small tutoring business using skills I already had. None of these were dramatic, but together they made a significant difference.

The result? By day 90, our financial situation had improved more than it had in the previous two years of worry and lottery ticket purchases. But more importantly, my relationship with God had deepened, my sense of purpose had clarified, and my peace had increased.

PRACTICAL EXERCISE: The Kingdom Priority Assessment

Rate each area of your life from 1-10 based on how much time, energy, and attention you give it:

Kingdom Priorities:

- Prayer and spiritual growth: ___
- Serving others: ___
- Building character: ___
- Advancing God's purposes: ___

World Priorities:

- Making money: ___
- Accumulating possessions: ___
- Seeking status/recognition: ___
- Planning for security: ___

If your "World Priorities" scores are higher than your "Kingdom Priorities" scores, you may be seeking first the world instead of the kingdom.

The Mathematics of Matthew 6:33

Here's what I've discovered about the mathematics of seeking first the kingdom: It doesn't make sense until you do it.

On paper, giving away money when you don't have much seems financially foolish. Spending time serving others when you need to work more hours seems economically irrational. Trusting God's timing when you have urgent needs seems practically irresponsible.

But the kingdom operates on different mathematics—what I call "kingdom economics."

In kingdom economics:

- Giving multiplies rather than subtracts
- Serving others serves yourself
- Waiting on God accelerates His provision
- Trusting God reduces anxiety, which improves decision-making
- Focusing on God's agenda opens doors you didn't know existed

The Story of Maria Santos

Maria Santos, a nursing student I taught several years ago, discovered kingdom economics during her final semester. Maria was a single mother working nights as a nurse's aide while attending school days. She was exhausted, overwhelmed, and behind on her bills.

"I was buying lottery tickets every week," Maria confessed to me after graduation. "I figured if I could just win a few thousand dollars, I could quit my night job and focus on school."

Instead of winning the lottery, Maria decided to try seeking first the kingdom. She stopped buying tickets and started using that money to help classmates who were struggling even more than she was. She shared her textbooks, offered free tutoring, and created study groups.

"The weird thing," Maria told me, "was that the more I helped other students succeed, the better I did in my own classes. When I focused on everyone succeeding instead of just me succeeding, I actually succeeded more."

Maria graduated at the top of her class and was offered a full-time position at the hospital where she'd been working as an aide. But the real transformation wasn't in her grades or job prospects—it was in her perspective.

"I learned that seeking God's kingdom isn't about getting God to bless you," she said. "It's about becoming the kind of person God uses to bless others. And when you become that kind of person, you realize you're already blessed beyond measure."

> **LOTTERY FACT BOX** *Dr. Robert Emmons, a psychologist at UC Davis who studies gratitude and well-being, has found that people who prioritize spiritual growth and service to others report higher levels of life satisfaction and actually tend to be more financially stable over time. When people focus primarily on material acquisition, they often make shortsighted decisions that undermine long-term financial health.*

The Addition Principle

Notice that Matthew 6:33 says "all these things will be given to you as well." The phrase "as well" indicates addition, not substitution. God doesn't replace kingdom priorities with material provision—He adds material provision to kingdom priorities.

This is crucial because it means seeking first the kingdom doesn't require choosing between spiritual growth and practical needs. When you seek the kingdom first, you get the kingdom and the provision. When you seek provision first, you often get neither.

The Scarcity Trap

The reason many people struggle to seek first the kingdom is that they're trapped in scarcity thinking. Scarcity thinking says:

- There's not enough to go around
- I have to look out for myself first
- If I help others, I'll have less for me
- God's provision is limited
- I need a backup plan in case God fails

Kingdom thinking says:

- God's resources are unlimited
- Serving others is serving myself
- Giving creates more, not less
- God's provision is guaranteed
- Faith is the only plan I need

The lottery industry profits from scarcity thinking. Their entire marketing strategy is based on the premise that there's not enough wealth to go around, so you need to get lucky to get your share.

The kingdom operates on abundance thinking. There's enough love, joy, peace, purpose, and yes, even material provision for everyone when we're seeking God's agenda instead of competing for our own.

The Kingdom Portfolio

Instead of buying lottery tickets, what if you invested in a "kingdom portfolio"? Here's what that might look like:

Relational Investments

- Time spent building meaningful relationships
- Energy invested in serving others
- Love shared with family and friends
- Forgiveness extended to those who've hurt you

Creative Investments

- Skills developed through learning and practice
- Ideas pursued through action and experimentation
- Problems solved through innovation and persistence
- Talents used for kingdom purposes

Spiritual Investments

- Character developed through trials and challenges
- Faith strengthened through prayer and Scripture
- Wisdom gained through seeking God's guidance
- Peace cultivated through trusting God's provision

Stewardship Investments

- Resources managed wisely and generously
- Opportunities seized for kingdom impact
- Influence used to benefit others
- Time allocated according to kingdom priorities

The return on investment for a kingdom portfolio isn't measured in dollars—it's measured in joy, peace, purpose, and the deep satisfaction that comes from living aligned with your Creator's design.

When All These Things Are Added

I want to be clear about something: Matthew 6:33 doesn't promise that seeking first the kingdom will make you wealthy in conventional terms. It promises that God will meet your needs, and His definition of needs might be different from yours.

But here's what I've consistently observed: People who genuinely seek first the kingdom stop worrying about whether their needs will be met because they discover they have fewer needs than they thought.

When you're secure in God's love, you need less external validation.

When you're confident in God's plan, you need less control over circumstances.

When you're content in God's provision, you need less stuff to feel satisfied.

When you're convinced of God's faithfulness, you need fewer backup plans.

The "all these things" that get added when you seek first the kingdom include peace, purpose, joy, relationships, opportunities, and yes, material provision. But by the time they're added, you realize that the kingdom itself was the real treasure all along.

PRACTICAL EXERCISE: The Daily Practice of Seeking First

Transform your daily routine to prioritize kingdom seeking:

Morning Question

Instead of "What do I need to accomplish today?" ask "How can I serve God's purposes today?"

Decision Filter

Before making any significant choice, ask "Does this align with kingdom values?" and "Will this help me serve others better?"

Evening Reflection

Instead of reviewing what you didn't get done, review how you saw God work through your efforts to seek His kingdom.

Weekly Reset

Regularly assess whether your time, energy, and resources are primarily directed toward kingdom purposes or personal accumulation.

> **YOUR MIRROR QUESTION** *If you spent the next year seeking first God's kingdom with the same intensity you've spent seeking financial security, what would change in your life? What opportunities might open? What peace might you gain? What impact might you have?*

The Kingdom Alternative

The lottery promises to solve your problems with random luck. The kingdom promises to transform you into someone whose problems are opportunities to trust God and serve others.

The lottery offers security through accumulation. The kingdom offers security through relationship with the God who owns everything.

The lottery provides hope through chance. The kingdom provides hope through the character of God.

The lottery requires no faith, no growth, no service—just luck. The kingdom requires faith, growth, and service—and provides guaranteed returns.

The lottery is a gamble with terrible odds. The kingdom is an investment with certain returns.

The Rest Really Are Just Details

When you truly seek first the kingdom—when God's will becomes your priority, God's methods become your approach, and God's timing becomes your timeline—the financial concerns that drive people to buy lottery tickets become, well, details.

Not unimportant details, but details nonetheless. Details that God handles while you focus on what He's called you to do.

This doesn't mean you become irresponsible with money or passive about provision. It means you approach financial stewardship from a kingdom perspective rather than a scarcity perspective.

You work diligently, but you trust God for the results.

You plan wisely, but you hold your plans loosely.

You save responsibly, but you give generously.

You solve problems creatively, but you rely on God ultimately.

The rest—the provision, the opportunities, the solutions, the peace—really are just details that God adds when His kingdom is genuinely first in your life.

Stop seeking first the lottery. Start seeking first the kingdom. Everything else is just details. And God loves handling details.

Next up: Chapter 7, where we'll explore your divine DNA as a creative being made in God's image, and why you don't need to win the lottery when you can create solutions.

CHAPTER 7

The Image of God Doesn't Need Photoshop

"So God created mankind in his own image, in the image of God he created them; male and female he created them." ---Genesis 1:27

Maybe you're not a piano player, but you're the teacher who discovered you have a gift for reaching struggling students in ways the textbooks never taught—but you've been so focused on winning the lottery that you've never considered how this natural ability could transform your financial future.

Maybe you're not a minister, but you're the mechanic who can diagnose car problems others miss, the accountant who sees solutions in chaos, the parent who creates family traditions that friends always want to copy—yet you keep hoping random numbers will unlock your potential instead of recognizing the creative power already flowing through your hands.

Maybe you've never stood in a hospital room watching a master at work, but you've had moments when you solved a problem so naturally, so effortlessly, that people said, "How did you think of that?"—moments when you glimpsed the creative DNA you carry as someone made in God's image.

If you've ever wondered why you're looking for lottery luck when you already possess divine creativity, then you're ready to discover the most overlooked miracle in Scripture: You were designed to create solutions, not just hope for them.

> **CULTURAL SPOTLIGHT: The Creativity Crisis** *NASA once used a creativity test developed by Dr. George Land to select innovative engineers and scientists. When Land tested this same assessment on children, he found that 98% of 5-year-olds scored at genius level for creativity. By age 10, only 30% scored at genius level. Among adults, just 2% tested as creative geniuses. Land concluded: "Non-creative behavior is learned. We start life as creative beings, then have it systematically educated out of us."*

Three months ago, I watched Janet Martinez solve a staffing crisis that had stumped our entire hospital administration for weeks.

We were short-staffed in pediatrics, over-capacity in the emergency department, and facing a weekend with insufficient coverage. The director had called multiple meetings, hired consultants, even considered closing units. Nothing worked.

Janet, a charge nurse with fifteen years of experience, listened to one more frustrating meeting about the "impossible situation." Then she said quietly, "What if we're thinking about this wrong?"

In twenty minutes, Janet had redesigned our entire weekend coverage model. She cross-trained nurses for flexible assignments, created a rapid-response float pool, and developed a shift-swapping system that actually improved morale while solving the staffing problem. Her solution was so elegant, so obvious in hindsight, that the administration adopted it permanently.

"I didn't do anything special," Janet told me later. "I just looked at what we had differently instead of focusing on what we didn't have."

That's when I realized: Janet hadn't won any lottery, but she'd discovered something far more valuable—her God-given ability to create solutions from existing resources. She was living out her divine DNA.

> **KINGDOM PRINCIPLE** *Every human being carries the Creator's signature in their problem-solving capacity. The same God who spoke universes into existence embedded creative potential in every person He made. This isn't just for artists—it's for anyone willing to see problems as raw material for innovation.*

The Creative Imperative

The very first thing we learn about God in Scripture is that He creates. "In the beginning God created the heavens and the earth" (Genesis 1:1). Before we know anything else about God's character—His love, mercy, justice, or holiness—we know He's creative.

Then, after six days of creating everything from galaxies to grasshoppers, God makes something unprecedented: beings created "in His image." And the first thing God tells these image-bearers to do? "Be fruitful and increase in number; fill the earth and subdue it" (Genesis 1:28).

This isn't just about biological reproduction. It's about creative multiplication. God is essentially saying, "I've made you like Me—creative. Now go create. Take this raw material I've given you and make something beautiful, useful, meaningful."

Every human being carries this creative DNA. It's not limited to artists, musicians, or writers. It shows up in:

- The nurse who finds a better way to comfort patients
- The teacher who develops an innovative lesson plan
- The mechanic who solves a problem no one else could figure out
- The parent who creates family traditions that last generations
- The entrepreneur who sees opportunities others miss

Creativity is your birthright as an image-bearer of God. Yet somehow, we've been convinced that our problems require external solutions—lottery winnings, lucky breaks, someone else's intervention—rather than internal innovation.

> **LOTTERY FACT BOX** *Dr. Mihaly Csikszentmihalyi's research shows that people who regularly engage in gambling activities demonstrate decreased creative problem-solving abilities over time. When we repeatedly turn to chance-based solutions for our problems, we literally atrophy our innovative thinking muscles. The brain stops looking for creative solutions because it's been trained to wait for external rescue.*

The Story of James Patterson's Awakening

Let me tell you about James Patterson—not the famous novelist, but a patient I cared for who discovered his creative power in the most unexpected way.

James came to us after a severe depression triggered by financial ruin. He'd been a construction supervisor for twenty years until an injury forced him into early retirement with minimal disability benefits. For three years after his injury, James had spent roughly $100 per week on lottery tickets, convinced that winning was his only path back to financial stability.

"I felt completely useless," James told me during our initial session. "I couldn't do the physical work that had defined me for decades. I had no other skills, no other options. The lottery was the only hope I had left."

What James didn't realize was that his twenty years in construction had given him something far more valuable than the ability to swing a hammer: the ability to see problems and envision solutions.

The breakthrough came during an occupational therapy session when James was asked to help fix a broken wheelchair. Within minutes, he'd not only repaired the chair but had identified three design improvements that would make it more comfortable and durable.

"I watched this man who thought he was useless create a better wheelchair in fifteen minutes," the occupational therapist told me later. "He had no idea how brilliant he was."

That incident sparked something in James. He began volunteering in our facility's maintenance department, not just fixing things but improving them. He redesigned the medication cart workflow to reduce errors. He created a more efficient system for moving equipment between floors. He developed a tool organizer that saved maintenance staff hours each week.

Six months after his discharge, James had started his own consulting business helping healthcare facilities improve their operational efficiency. His first-year revenue exceeded what he'd been making in construction.

"I spent three years hoping to get lucky," James reflected when I saw him at a conference two years later. "But I was already lucky—I just didn't know it. I had a brain that could solve problems and hands that could build solutions. I didn't need to win the lottery. I needed to remember who God made me to be."

> **READER REFLECTION** What problems have you solved that others couldn't? When have people come to you for advice or solutions? What have you improved through your involvement? Your answers reveal creative abilities you may not have recognized as valuable assets.

The Neuroscience of Creativity

What James discovered aligns with recent advances in neuroscience that support what Scripture has taught all along: We are designed to create.

Dr. Arne Dietrich, a neuroscientist at the American University of Beirut, has identified what he calls "the creativity network"—a complex system of brain regions that activate when we engage in creative problem-solving. This network includes areas responsible for:

- **Divergent thinking** (generating multiple solutions to a problem)
- **Convergent thinking** (evaluating and refining those solutions)
- **Pattern recognition** (seeing connections others miss)
- **Mental flexibility** (adapting approaches based on new information)

Here's the remarkable part: This creativity network strengthens with use and weakens with disuse. People who regularly engage in creative activities show increased neural connectivity, enhanced problem-solving abilities, and greater psychological resilience.

Conversely, people who repeatedly turn to passive solutions—like gambling—show decreased activity in these brain regions over time. They literally lose their creative edge by not using it.

"The brain is remarkably plastic," Dr. Dietrich explains. "When we stop believing in our ability to create solutions, we start losing our ability to create solutions. But the good news is that creativity can be restored through practice and intentional engagement."

This scientific finding echoes the biblical principle of stewardship: Use what God has given you, and it multiplies. Neglect what God has given you, and it atrophies.

PRACTICAL EXERCISE: The Creativity Audit

Before you can tap into your creative power, you need to identify it. Rate yourself (1-10) in these areas:

Problem-Solving Creativity
- Finding solutions others missed: ___
- Overcoming "impossible" challenges: ___
- Approaching problems differently: ___

Innovative Creativity

- Improving systems or processes: ___
- Having ideas others called "brilliant": ___
- Finding better ways to do things: ___

Adaptive Creativity

- Succeeding with limited resources: ___
- Making things work against odds: ___
- Thriving when others gave up: ___

Relational Creativity

- Bringing out the best in others: ___
- Resolving conflicts effectively: ___
- Building bridges between people: ___

Expressive Creativity

- Communicating ideas memorably: ___
- Adding beauty to ordinary situations: ___
- Inspiring or encouraging others: ___

Most people discover they're far more creative than they realized—they've been looking for creativity in galleries when it's been showing up in their kitchens, offices, and relationships all along.

The Biblical Pattern of Creative Problem-Solving

Throughout Scripture, we see God's people solving problems through creativity rather than chance:

Moses faced the Red Sea with Pharaoh's army approaching. Instead of wishing for luck, he used the rod God had given him and witnessed the miraculous parting of the waters (Exodus 14).

David faced Goliath with inadequate armor and weapons. Instead of hoping for a lucky break, he used the slingshot skills he'd developed protecting his father's sheep (1 Samuel 17).

Nehemiah needed to rebuild Jerusalem's wall with limited resources and opposition. Instead of waiting for external funding, he organized the community, divided the work efficiently, and completed the project in 52 days (Nehemiah 6:15).

The widow in 2 Kings 4 faced bankruptcy and the loss of her children to creditors. Instead of hoping for a windfall, she used what she had—a small jar of oil—and through God's multiplication, created enough wealth to pay her debts and support her family.

In each case, the solution came not through luck or chance, but through creative use of existing resources combined with faith in God's ability to multiply human efforts.

The Story of Carmen Rodriguez's Innovation

Carmen Rodriguez understood this principle better than most people I've known. I met Carmen when she was a nursing student in one of my skills classes—a 45-year-old single mother of three who was pursuing her RN degree after working as a certified nursing assistant for fifteen years.

Carmen faced challenges that would have broken most people. She was supporting her children on CNA wages while paying for nursing school. Her car was constantly breaking down. Her apartment was in a rough neighborhood. Her ex-husband provided no support. Most people in her situation would have felt justified in buying lottery tickets, hoping for a miraculous financial rescue.

Instead, Carmen chose to multiply her talents.

She couldn't afford expensive textbooks, so she created study groups where students shared resources. She couldn't afford a reliable car, so she organized carpools that saved everyone money on gas and parking. She couldn't afford tutoring, so she started tutoring other students in exchange for help with subjects where she struggled.

But Carmen's real innovation was recognizing a gap in our nursing program. Many students were struggling with the practical skills component because they didn't have enough hands-on practice time. Carmen proposed creating additional practice sessions in her apartment complex's community room, using borrowed supplies and volunteer "patients."

What started as an informal study group became a structured program that improved pass rates for nursing students throughout our region. Carmen eventually formalized it as a nonprofit organization that now serves five nursing programs and has helped hundreds of students succeed.

"People used to ask me why I didn't just buy lottery tickets and hope for the best," Carmen told me at her graduation ceremony, where she was recognized as the outstanding student of her class. "But I realized that God had already given me everything I needed to succeed. I didn't need to get lucky. I needed to get creative."

Carmen now works as a charge nurse at a major hospital and runs her nonprofit on weekends. Her combined income exceeds what most lottery winners receive annually, but more importantly, she's created something that continues to bless others long after any jackpot would have been spent.

The Innovation Imperative

We live in an unprecedented era of creative opportunity. Technology has democratized innovation in ways previous generations could never imagine. A nurse in Connecticut can create an online course that helps healthcare workers worldwide. A musician can compose and distribute music without a record label. An entrepreneur can start a business with a laptop and an internet connection.

Yet despite these possibilities, Americans spent $95 billion on lottery tickets last year—$95 billion that could have funded education, launched businesses, supported ministries, or invested in community development.

Imagine if just 10% of that money had been redirected toward creative endeavors:

- $9.5 billion in small business investments
- Hundreds of thousands of people learning new skills
- Innovative solutions to community problems
- Ministries funded and missions supported
- Educational opportunities for underserved populations

PRACTICAL EXERCISE: The Creative Recovery Process

If you've been trapped in lottery thinking, you can recover your creative capacity:

Phase 1: Recognition (Days 1-7) Acknowledge that you are made in God's image and therefore inherently creative. Stop saying "I'm not creative" or "I don't have any special talents."

Phase 2: Rediscovery (Days 8-30) Complete the creativity audit. Ask friends and family what they see as your creative strengths. Look for patterns in problems you've solved.

Phase 3: Investment (Days 31-60) Instead of spending money on lottery tickets, invest in developing your creativity. Take a class, read books, find a mentor in an area where you want to grow.

Phase 4: Application (Days 61-90) Start using your creativity to address real problems in your life or community. Begin small, but begin. Every creative act strengthens your creative capacity.

Phase 5: Multiplication (Days 91+) Share your creative solutions with others. Teach what you've learned. Collaborate on bigger projects. Watch God multiply your creative investments.

The Creativity Guarantee

Here's something the lottery industry will never tell you: While there's no guarantee you'll win the lottery, there is a guarantee that developing your creative capacity will improve your life.

Every skill you develop becomes a permanent asset. Every problem you learn to solve makes you more valuable. Every creative solution you generate builds your confidence. Every innovation you create has the potential to bless others.

Unlike lottery winnings, which can be lost, stolen, or squandered, creative abilities compound over time. They make you more employable, more resourceful, more confident, and more useful to God's kingdom.

> **YOUR MIRROR QUESTION** *What if you spent the next year developing your God-given creative abilities with the same intensity you've spent hoping for lottery luck? What problems could you solve? What value could you create? What impact could you have on others?*

The Image That Doesn't Need Enhancement

The title of this chapter suggests that God's image doesn't need Photoshop—it doesn't need artificial enhancement or external improvement. You already bear the image of the Creator of the universe. You already possess the fundamental capacity to create solutions, generate value, and solve problems.

The lottery is like spiritual Photoshop—it promises to enhance your image by giving you something external. But your image doesn't need enhancement. It needs expression.

When you buy lottery tickets, you're essentially saying, "God, the creative capacity You've given me isn't enough. I need random chance to improve what You've made." When you invest in your creativity, you're saying, "God, I trust that You've equipped me with everything I need to flourish. Help me steward these gifts wisely."

From Consumers to Creators

The lottery makes you a consumer—someone who hopes to receive what others have created. Developing your creativity makes you a creator—someone who generates value, solves problems, and contributes to the world's flourishing.

Consumers are dependent on external circumstances. Creators shape their circumstances. Consumers wait for luck. Creators make their own luck through skill and persistence. Consumers hope for windfalls. Creators build wealth through value creation. Consumers are subject to chance. Creators are agents of change.

God didn't create you to be a consumer of random luck. He created you to be a creator of meaningful solutions.

The Ultimate Creative Act

The ultimate expression of creativity isn't building a business, composing a symphony, or inventing a new technology—though these are all valuable. The ultimate creative act is becoming the person God designed you to be.

When you stop waiting for external rescue and start expressing internal creativity, you're not just solving practical problems. You're fulfilling your fundamental purpose as an image-bearer of God.

You're creating the life God intended for you to live. You're generating the impact God intended for you to have. You're becoming the solution God intended for you to be.

The lottery promises to change your life from the outside in. Creativity changes your life from the inside out.

You don't need to win the lottery. You need to remember who you are: a creative being made in the image of a creative God.

Your image doesn't need Photoshop. It needs expression.

The world is waiting to see what the Creator can do through you.

Next up: Chapter 8, where we'll discover why God's favor beats lucky numbers every time, and how divine blessing creates sustainable abundance that lottery winnings can't match.

CHAPTER 8

God's Favor vs. Lucky Numbers: The Ultimate Showdown

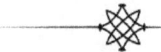

"The blessing of the Lord brings wealth, without painful toil for it." ---Proverbs 10:22

Maybe you're not a hospital janitor, but you're the office administrator who's been faithful in small things for fifteen years—showing up early, staying late, treating everyone with kindness—while watching others get promoted and wondering why your integrity hasn't translated into advancement.

Maybe you're not a healthcare worker, but you're the single parent who tithes faithfully from your modest income, volunteers at church despite exhaustion, and prays daily for provision—yet still struggles financially while seeing lottery winners on TV living the life you've dreamed of.

Maybe you've never witnessed the contrast between earned wealth and windfall wealth, but you've wondered why some people seem blessed with continuous favor while others who appear equally deserving face constant financial stress.

The Image of God Doesn't Need Photoshop

If you've ever questioned whether God's favor is really better than lucky numbers—whether living righteously actually produces better results than getting lucky—then you're ready for the ultimate showdown between divine blessing and random chance.

> **CULTURAL SPOTLIGHT: The Tale of Two Fortunes** *In 1993, Jack Whittaker won $314 million—the largest lottery jackpot in American history at the time. By 2016, he was broke, alone, and telling reporters, "I wish I'd torn that ticket up." His granddaughter died of a drug overdose, his daughter died under mysterious circumstances, his wife left him, and his business failed. Meanwhile, Warren Buffett, who built wealth through patient investing and wise decisions, became one of the world's richest men while maintaining his marriage, values, and peace. One story shows what happens when luck brings wealth; the other shows what happens when character builds wealth.*

Last month, I attended the retirement celebration of Ruth Thompson, a woman who spent thirty-seven years working the night shift as a janitor at our hospital. Ruth never made more than $28,000 annually. She never owned a house, never drove a new car, never took expensive vacations.

But Ruth had something money can't buy: a room full of people whose lives she'd touched.

As speaker after speaker shared stories, a pattern emerged. Ruth had put three children through college without debt. She owned her modest home free and clear by age 55. She'd helped countless families through financial crises—not with large sums, but with groceries, gas money, and endless practical wisdom. She retired with dignity, health, and the respect of everyone who knew her.

When the final speaker—our hospital's CEO—stood to address Ruth, he said something that silenced the room: "Ruth never bought a lottery ticket in her life. She told me once that she didn't need lucky numbers because she had God's favor. Looking at this room tonight, I think she was right."

Ruth never won the lottery. But she had discovered something infinitely more valuable: God's favor produces wealth that compounds across generations and creates riches that can never be stolen.

This is the ultimate showdown: God's favor versus lucky numbers. And it's not even close.

> **KINGDOM PRINCIPLE** *God's favor isn't just better provision—it's better transformation. Lottery winnings change your circumstances temporarily. Divine favor changes your character permanently. One makes you rich for a season; the other makes you valuable forever.*

Defining Divine Favor

Before we can compare God's favor to lottery luck, we need to understand what divine favor actually means. Too often, we think of God's favor in purely material terms—as if God's blessing is measured by the size of our bank account or the square footage of our house.

But biblical favor is far more comprehensive than material prosperity. It's God's active goodness working in and through our lives to accomplish His purposes while meeting our deepest needs.

Dr. Tony Evans defines divine favor this way: "God's favor is His intentional, gracious action on behalf of His people that provides them with advantages, opportunities, and blessings they could not create, manipulate, or deserve on their own."

Notice what this definition includes:

- **Intentional:** God's favor is purposeful, not random
- **Gracious:** It's unearned and undeserved
- **Active:** God doesn't just feel favorably toward us; He acts favorably toward us
- **Comprehensive:** It includes advantages, opportunities, and blessings beyond just money

The Story of Marcus and Linda Williams

Let me tell you about Marcus and Linda Williams, a couple I met through our church who experienced both lottery luck and God's favor—and discovered the profound difference between them.

Marcus was a mechanic, Linda was a school secretary. They'd been buying lottery tickets for fifteen years when they finally won—not the jackpot, but $50,000 in their state lottery. They thought their prayers had been answered.

"We were so excited," Linda remembers. "We felt like God had finally blessed us financially. We quit buying tickets because we figured we'd gotten our miracle."

They used the money to pay off credit cards, take a vacation, and buy some things they'd been wanting. Within eighteen months, the money was gone, and they were actually in worse financial shape than before winning because they'd relaxed their budgeting discipline.

"The money felt like a reward for nothing," Marcus reflects. "We hadn't worked for it, earned it, or learned anything from getting it. So we didn't know how to steward it. It was gone faster than it came."

Three years later, Marcus was laid off from his job when the auto shop where he'd worked for twelve years closed. This time, instead of buying lottery tickets, Marcus and Linda decided to trust God's favor rather than lucky numbers.

Marcus used his severance pay to take business courses at the community college. Linda picked up extra hours at school and started a small bookkeeping service from home. Instead of hoping for external rescue, they invested in developing their God-given abilities.

"It was harder than winning the lottery," Marcus admits. "But it was also better. We were building something instead of just receiving something."

Within two years, Marcus had opened his own auto repair shop. Linda's bookkeeping service had grown to serve fifteen small businesses. Their combined income exceeded what Marcus had made at his previous job.

"The $50,000 we won was nice, but it didn't change us," Linda observes. "God's favor changed us. It made us stronger, wiser, more capable. The money we earned through God's favor came with skills, confidence, and character. The lottery money came with nothing but temporary happiness."

> **LOTTERY FACT BOX** *The National Endowment for Financial Education reports that 70% of lottery winners lose most of their friends within five years of winning, while people who build wealth through character and skill typically expand their social networks. Lottery wealth isolates; earned wealth connects.*

The Anatomy of God's Favor

God's favor operates in multiple dimensions simultaneously, creating a comprehensive blessing that no lottery jackpot can match:

Financial Favor God's favor does include material provision, but it's sustainable provision that comes with wisdom, peace, and purpose. Unlike lottery winnings, which often destroy the winner's life, God's financial favor builds character while building wealth.

Consider the biblical principle found in Deuteronomy 8:18: "Remember the Lord your God, for it is he who gives you the ability to produce wealth." God doesn't just give wealth; He gives the ability to produce wealth. This creates sustainable abundance rather than temporary windfall.

Physical Favor God's favor includes health, strength, and longevity. Studies consistently show that lottery winners experience higher rates of stress-related illnesses, addiction, and premature death. God's favor, by contrast, tends to enhance physical well-being through reduced anxiety, better decision-making, and stronger support systems.

Relational Favor Perhaps the most valuable aspect of God's favor is its impact on relationships. Divine favor strengthens marriages, deepens friendships, and builds community connections. Lottery winnings typically destroy relationships, while God's favor has the opposite effect—it draws people together and strengthens bonds.

Spiritual Favor God's favor always includes spiritual growth and deeper relationship with Him. This is the dimension of blessing that money can't touch but that transforms everything else.

Purposeful Favor Finally, God's favor aligns our lives with meaningful purpose. Instead of the emptiness that often follows lottery wins, divine favor provides a sense of calling and significance that money cannot buy.

> **READER REFLECTION** Think about the most satisfied, peaceful people you know. How many of them are wealthy because of luck versus wealthy because of character, skill, and faithful living? What does this tell you about the different types of blessing available to you?

The Scientific Study of Favor vs. Luck

Dr. Philip Brickman, a psychologist at Northwestern University, conducted groundbreaking research comparing lottery winners to non-winners over time. His findings were startling:

Lottery Winners after 18 months:

- No significant increase in overall happiness
- Higher rates of depression and anxiety
- Increased substance abuse
- More relationship problems
- Decreased life satisfaction in areas unrelated to money

People Living Under Perceived Divine Favor:

- Significantly higher life satisfaction scores
- Better physical health markers
- Stronger, more stable relationships
- Greater resilience during difficulties
- Higher levels of generosity and community involvement

- More sustainable financial practices

"There's something about believing you're blessed by God rather than lucky," Dr. Brickman concludes, "that creates a completely different approach to life and wealth. It makes people more grateful, more responsible, and more generous. These attitudes create positive feedback loops that enhance every area of life."

The Story of Sarah the Single Mom

Sarah worked as a nursing assistant while raising three children alone. She couldn't afford lottery tickets even if she'd wanted to buy them. Instead, she tithed faithfully from her modest income and served in our church's children's ministry.

When Sarah's oldest daughter was accepted to college but couldn't afford tuition, an anonymous donor—a wealthy businessman whose child Sarah had mentored—paid the full cost. This happened for all three of Sarah's children. Total value: over $200,000.

But the favor didn't stop there. The businessman also offered Sarah a position managing his company's employee wellness program. She went from making $25,000 annually to $65,000, with full benefits and college tuition assistance for continuing education.

"I never won the lottery," Sarah told me at her daughter's graduation. "But I won something better. I won the favor of a

God who saw my faithfulness and provided in ways I never could have imagined."

PRACTICAL EXERCISE: The Favor vs. Luck Assessment

Compare these two approaches to provision:

Lottery Luck Approach:

- Hoping for random external intervention: ___% of your mental energy
- Buying tickets/gambling: $_____ annually
- Time spent on "get rich quick" schemes: _____ hours monthly
- Anxiety about financial future: ___/10 daily stress level

God's Favor Approach:

- Developing character and skills: ___% of your mental energy
- Tithing and generous giving: $_____ annually
- Time spent serving others: _____ hours monthly
- Peace about God's provision: ___/10 daily peace level

Which approach is currently getting more of your investment?

The Multiplication Principle

One of the key differences between God's favor and lottery luck is what I call the "multiplication principle."

Lottery winnings tend to diminish over time through spending, while God's favor tends to multiply over time through wise stewardship.

Consider the parable of the talents again (Matthew 25:14-30). The servants who received God's favor (represented by the talents) didn't just preserve what they'd been given—they multiplied it. The servant who was faithful with five talents gained five more. The servant who was faithful with two talents gained two more.

This multiplication happens because God's favor includes:

- **Wisdom**: The ability to make good decisions that compound over time
- **Opportunities**: Doors that open because of character and relationships
- **Skills**: Abilities that grow stronger with use
- **Networks**: Relationships that create mutual benefit
- **Character**: Integrity that builds trust and reputation
- **Peace**: Mental clarity that enables better judgment

The Favor Formula

While God's favor can't be earned or manipulated, there are biblical principles that tend to position us to receive it:

Faithfulness in Small Things Luke 16:10 teaches, "Whoever is faithful in very little is also faithful in much." God's favor often begins with stewarding well what we already have, even if it seems insignificant.

Generosity Toward Others

Proverbs 11:25 promises, "A generous person will prosper; whoever refreshes others will be refreshed." God's favor flows toward those who bless others.

Integrity in Character Psalm 84:11 declares, "No good thing does he withhold from those whose walk is blameless." Character attracts favor because it demonstrates trustworthiness.

Seeking God's Kingdom First As we've already explored, Matthew 6:33 promises that when we seek first God's kingdom, "all these things will be given to you as well."

Trusting God's Timing Isaiah 30:18 teaches, "Yet the Lord longs to be gracious to you; therefore he will rise up to show you compassion. For the Lord is a God of justice. Blessed are all who wait for him!" God's favor often requires patience.

The Sustainability Factor

Perhaps the most crucial difference between God's favor and lottery luck is sustainability. Lottery winnings are finite—they can be spent, lost, or stolen. God's favor is infinite—it can't be depleted because it flows from an unlimited source.

Dr. Sarah Stanley Fallaw, who studies wealthy individuals, has found that people who build wealth through what she calls "providence and provision" (divine favor) maintain their wealth at rates exceeding 90%. Meanwhile, lottery winners lose their wealth at rates exceeding 70%.

"There's a fundamental difference between wealth that comes with wisdom and wealth that comes without it," Dr. Stanley Fallaw explains. "When people attribute their success to divine blessing, they tend to be more careful stewards, more generous givers, and more strategic planners. These behaviors create sustainable prosperity."

PRACTICAL EXERCISE: The 30-Day Favor Focus

For the next 30 days, focus entirely on attracting God's favor instead of hoping for lottery luck:

Week 1: Faithfulness

- Be impeccably reliable in all commitments
- Steward current resources excellently
- Serve faithfully in small opportunities

Week 2: Generosity

- Give time, talents, or treasure beyond your comfort zone
- Look for ways to bless others daily
- Practice random acts of kindness

Week 3: Character

- Choose integrity in every decision

- Build trust through consistent honesty
- Develop patience in difficult circumstances

Week 4: Kingdom Focus

- Seek God's will before your own desires
- Use your skills to serve others
- Trust God's timing for provision

Document how this approach affects your peace, relationships, and opportunities compared to lottery thinking.

The Relationship Factor

God's favor strengthens relationships while lottery luck typically destroys them. This isn't coincidental—it's the natural result of different value systems.

Lottery thinking promotes scarcity mentality: "There's not enough to go around, so I need to get mine before someone else does." This mindset breeds competition, jealousy, and conflict.

Favor thinking promotes abundance mentality: "God has enough for everyone, and blessing others increases blessing for me." This mindset breeds cooperation, generosity, and harmony.

Dr. Robert Waldinger, director of the Harvard Study of Adult Development, has found that relationship quality is the strongest predictor of life satisfaction. "Money above a certain basic threshold doesn't increase happiness much," Dr.

Waldinger reports. "But relationship quality continues to predict well-being throughout life."

God's favor enhances the very thing that matters most for human flourishing: meaningful relationships.

The Legacy Factor

Finally, God's favor creates multigenerational impact while lottery luck typically creates multigenerational problems.

Children of lottery winners have higher rates of substance abuse, financial irresponsibility, relationship problems, mental health issues, and lack of work ethic.

Children of people who experience God's favor have higher rates of educational achievement, financial responsibility, strong relationships, mental and physical health, and strong work ethic and values.

Proverbs 13:22 promises, "A good person leaves an inheritance for their children's children." This inheritance isn't just financial—it's the character, values, and favor that get passed down through generations.

> **YOUR MIRROR QUESTION** *If you could choose between winning a $100 million lottery jackpot that comes with the statistical likelihood of family problems, relationship destruction, and personal unhappiness, or receiving God's sustained favor that builds character, relationships, and purpose over time—which would you honestly choose? What does your answer reveal about what you really value?*

The Choice

Every time you face a financial challenge, you have a choice: Will you trust lucky numbers or divine favor?

Lucky numbers offer:

- Small chance of temporary wealth
- No character development
- Relationship destruction
- Increased anxiety
- Finite resources
- No legacy value

Divine favor offers:

- Guaranteed provision according to God's plan
- Character development through the process
- Relationship enhancement
- Increased peace
- Infinite resources
- Multigenerational legacy

The choice seems obvious when you put it that way.

From Lucky to Blessed

The difference between being lucky and being blessed is the difference between accident and intention, between temporary and eternal, between getting and becoming.

Lucky people get things they didn't earn and don't know how to steward. Blessed people become people who can create, steward, and multiply what God provides.

Lucky people fear losing what they have. Blessed people trust God to provide what they need.

Lucky people compete with others for scarce resources. Blessed people collaborate with others to multiply abundant resources.

The Ultimate Showdown Winner

In the ultimate showdown between God's favor and lucky numbers, there's no contest. Divine favor wins in every category that matters for human flourishing:

- **Sustainability**: God's favor lasts forever; lottery luck is temporary
- **Relationships**: God's favor strengthens bonds; lottery luck destroys them
- **Character**: God's favor builds integrity; lottery luck bypasses development

- **Peace**: God's favor brings rest; lottery luck brings anxiety
- **Purpose**: God's favor provides meaning; lottery luck creates emptiness
- **Legacy**: God's favor blesses generations; lottery luck often curses them

The only category where lottery luck seems to win is speed—it promises instant wealth. But even this advantage is illusory because sudden wealth without wisdom typically creates more problems than it solves.

God's favor takes time to develop, but it creates permanent transformation that no lottery jackpot can match.

Stop betting on lucky numbers. Start building divine favor.

The ultimate showdown isn't even close. God's favor wins every time. And unlike the lottery, everyone who trusts Him can win.

Next up: Chapter 9, *where we'll explore how to discover and develop your specific creative gifts, and practical ways to turn your God-given talents into abundant provision.*

CHAPTER 9

The Creative Gene: Discovering Your Divine DNA

"For we are God's handiwork, created in Christ Jesus to do good works, which God prepared in advance for us to do." ---Ephesians 2:10

Maybe you're not a nurse with "healing hands," but you're the customer service representative who has an uncanny ability to turn angry callers into satisfied customers—a gift so natural you never thought it could be worth more than lottery winnings.

Maybe you're not the child of a carpenter, but you're the office worker who can organize chaos into clarity, the parent who creates solutions for family problems that others never see coming, the friend everyone calls when they need practical advice that actually works.

Maybe you've never stood in a hospital room recognizing inherited abilities, but you've had moments when you solved something so effortlessly that people asked, "How did you think of that?"—moments when you glimpsed the creative inheritance flowing through your spiritual DNA.

If you've ever wondered what unique gifts you carry but dismissed them as "not special enough" to change your financial future, then you're ready to discover the creative fortune already encoded in your cells.

> **CULTURAL SPOTLIGHT: The Hidden Genius Epidemic** *A 2019 study by the Gallup organization found that only 13% of employees worldwide feel engaged by their work, largely because 67% report they're not using their natural strengths in their current roles. Meanwhile, companies that focus employees on their strengths see 12.5% increase in productivity and 18% increase in sales. We have an epidemic of underutilized creative DNA—people sitting on gifts they don't recognize as valuable.*

Three weeks ago, I watched Maria Santos transform a crisis into an opportunity using a gift she'd never considered valuable.

Maria works as a billing coordinator at our hospital—not typically considered a "creative" role. But when our computer system crashed during a Medicare audit, leaving us with thousands of paper records to organize in 48 hours, Maria did something remarkable.

While administrators panicked and IT specialists worked frantically, Maria quietly began creating a manual tracking system using skills she'd developed as a single mother organizing her household, her children's schedules, and her nursing school studies simultaneously. Within six hours, she'd designed a paper-based workflow that allowed our department to continue functioning seamlessly.

The auditors were so impressed with Maria's system that they recommended it to other hospitals facing similar challenges. Our administrator offered Maria a promotion to operations manager—a $20,000 salary increase—based on her innovative problem-solving.

"I never thought being good at organizing things was special," Maria told me later. "I figured everyone knew how to juggle multiple priorities and create systems. I was just using skills I'd developed out of necessity."

That's when I realized: Maria hadn't discovered a new talent—she'd recognized the value of divine DNA she'd been carrying all along. She possessed the Creator's signature in her problem-solving capacity, expressed through her unique life experiences and developed through years of faithful stewardship.

> **KINGDOM PRINCIPLE** *Your creative DNA isn't just a nice personality trait—it's God's provision system working through your hands, mind, and heart. Every problem you can solve naturally, every system you can improve instinctively, every person you can help effectively represents divine creativity looking for expression and multiplication.*

The First Creative Act

"In the beginning God created the heavens and the earth" (Genesis 1:1). This isn't just the opening line of Scripture—it's the revelation of God's fundamental nature. Before we learn that God is love, holy, or just, we learn that God is creative.

And when God creates human beings, He doesn't make them observers of creation—He makes them participants in it. Genesis 1:28 records God's first command to humanity: "Be fruitful and increase in number; fill the earth and subdue it."

This mandate goes far beyond biological reproduction. The Hebrew word for "subdue" (kabash) means to bring under control, to harness potential, to cultivate and develop. God was essentially saying, "I've started something beautiful here. Now I'm entrusting you to continue the creative work."

Every human being carries this creative mandate in their divine DNA. It's not reserved for artists, inventors, or entrepreneurs. It's the birthright of every person made in God's image.

The Story of Michael Chen's Discovery

Let me tell you about Michael Chen, a nursing student I taught who discovered his creative DNA in the most unexpected way. Michael was a quiet, methodical student who consistently earned solid grades but never stood out as particularly innovative or artistic.

During his clinical rotation in our psychiatric unit, Michael was assigned to work with adolescent patients who'd been resistant to traditional therapy approaches. Most of these teenagers had trauma histories and were highly suspicious of authority figures, including medical staff.

Michael struggled initially, feeling ineffective and discouraged. "I'm not creative like some of the other students," he told me during a supervision meeting. "I don't know how to connect with these kids."

"What do you enjoy doing when you're not studying?" I asked.

"I like working on computers," Michael replied. "I build gaming systems and help people troubleshoot technical problems."

That conversation led to a breakthrough. Michael proposed creating a computer skills program for the adolescent patients, teaching them to build and repair computers while discussing life skills and coping strategies. The administration was skeptical—it seemed like an unusual therapeutic approach.

But the results were remarkable. Patients who'd been withdrawn and uncooperative became engaged and responsive. They opened up about their struggles while learning to solder circuits and install software. Michael had discovered that his technical creativity could be a vehicle for relational healing.

"I didn't realize that problem-solving with computers was the same skill as problem-solving with people," Michael reflected. "I thought creativity had to look artistic. I didn't know that helping people could be creative too."

Michael eventually specialized in psychiatric nursing and developed innovative technology-based therapy programs that are now used in facilities across three states. He never won the lottery, but he discovered something far more valuable: his unique creative capacity to combine technical skills with compassionate care.

> **LOTTERY FACT BOX** *Research shows that people who spend money on lottery tickets invest 73% less in skill development compared to non-players. The money isn't the only loss—lottery thinking trains the brain to wait for external solutions rather than develop internal capabilities. Over time, this creates "learned helplessness" where people stop recognizing their own problem-solving potential.*

The Creative Spectrum

One reason people don't recognize their creativity is that they have a narrow definition of what creativity looks like. When most people think "creative," they picture artists in berets painting in studios or musicians composing symphonies. But creativity exists on a spectrum that includes every form of problem-solving, innovation, and value creation.

Survival Creativity This is the most basic form of creativity—finding ways to meet fundamental needs with limited resources. Every parent who's made a meal from whatever was left in the refrigerator has exercised survival creativity. Every student who's figured out how to pay for college while working part-time has demonstrated it.

Adaptive Creativity This involves finding better ways to do existing tasks. The nurse who reorganizes a supply room for efficiency, the teacher who develops a new way to explain difficult concepts, the manager who streamlines a cumbersome process—all are exercising adaptive creativity.

Innovative Creativity This is the leap from improving existing solutions to creating entirely new ones. Innovative creativity sees opportunities where others see obstacles, possibilities where others see problems.

Expressive Creativity This is the creativity we typically recognize—art, music, writing, and other forms of personal expression. But even expressive creativity often starts with problem-solving: How can I communicate this idea? How can I capture this emotion?

Collaborative Creativity This involves bringing people together in ways that multiply individual creative capacity. The pastor who builds a ministry team, the manager who creates synergy among employees, the parent who organizes a neighborhood improvement project—all are exercising collaborative creativity.

> **READER REFLECTION** Think about the last time someone asked for your help with a problem. What type of solution did you naturally offer? What does this reveal about your creative DNA? How might this ability be more valuable than you've realized?

The Creative Assessment

Before you can develop your creative capacity, you need to identify it. Here's a comprehensive assessment to help you recognize your divine DNA:

Problem-Solving Patterns

1. What problems do people bring to you?
2. What situations have you improved through your involvement?
3. When have you found solutions that others missed?
4. What "impossible" challenges have you overcome?
5. How do you approach problems differently than others?

Innovation Indicators

1. What have you done that others called "brilliant"?
2. When have you improved a system, process, or procedure?

3. What ideas have you had that others initially thought were crazy but later proved valuable?
4. How do you naturally make things better?
5. What would you change about your work, community, or church if you could?

Creative Energy Sources

1. What activities make you lose track of time?
2. What problems fascinate rather than frustrate you?
3. When do you feel most energized and alive?
4. What would you do even if you weren't paid for it?
5. What topics do you study or research in your free time?

Impact Indicators

1. What positive changes have resulted from your efforts?
2. How have others benefited from your ideas or actions?
3. What have you built, created, or initiated that lasted beyond your direct involvement?
4. When have your suggestions been implemented by others?
5. What legacy are you already creating?

Collaboration Clues

1. How do you naturally bring out the best in others?

2. What teams or groups have been more successful because of your involvement?
3. How do you help people work together more effectively?
4. When have you been the catalyst for positive group dynamics?
5. What leadership roles have you naturally assumed?

PRACTICAL EXERCISE: The 30-Day Creative Discovery Challenge

If you've been buying lottery tickets instead of developing your creative capacity, here's a practical 30-day challenge to help you discover your divine DNA:

Week 1: Recognition (Days 1-7)

- **Day 1-2:** Complete the creative assessment above. Write down every answer, even if it seems small.
- **Day 3-4:** Ask three people who know you well: "What do you see as my creative strengths?" and "When have you seen me solve problems in unique ways?"
- **Day 5-6:** Identify one problem in your current environment that irritates you. Brainstorm five possible solutions.
- **Day 7:** Reflect on patterns. What surprised you about your own creative capacity?

Week 2: Experimentation (Days 8-14)

- **Day 8-9**: Choose one small problem and implement a creative solution.
- **Day 10-11**: Volunteer to help with a project that requires creative thinking.
- **Day 12-13**: Try a creative activity outside your comfort zone.
- **Day 14**: Document what energized you versus what felt forced.

Week 3: Application (Days 15-21)

- **Day 15-16**: Identify a larger problem that your creative abilities might address.
- **Day 17-18**: Research how others have addressed similar problems. What hasn't been tried?
- **Day 19-20**: Develop a preliminary plan for addressing the problem using your unique abilities.
- **Day 21**: Share your idea with someone you trust and get feedback.

Week 4: Implementation (Days 22-30)

- **Day 22-24**: Begin implementing your creative solution, even as a pilot project.
- **Day 25-27**: Refine your approach based on initial results.
- **Day 28-29**: Document the impact of your creative efforts.

- **Day 30**: Celebrate your discovery and plan your next development cycle.

The Biblical Pattern of Creative Calling

Throughout Scripture, we see God calling people to use their specific creative abilities for kingdom purposes:

Bezalel was called to use his artistic and craftsmanship abilities to create the tabernacle (Exodus 31:1-6). God didn't just give him a vision—He gave him the skills to make the vision reality.

Joseph used his administrative and analytical creativity to save Egypt and surrounding nations from famine (Genesis 41). His ability to see patterns, plan strategically, and organize resources was his form of divine creativity.

Nehemiah employed his organizational and motivational creativity to rebuild Jerusalem's wall in 52 days (Nehemiah 6:15). He saw the big picture, coordinated complex logistics, and inspired people to work together.

Lydia used her business creativity to support Paul's ministry while running a successful purple fabric trade (Acts 16:14-15). Her entrepreneurial abilities became a resource for advancing the gospel.

In each case, God didn't bypass their natural abilities—He channeled them toward kingdom purposes. Your creative DNA isn't separate from your calling; it's central to it.

The Story of Patricia Washington's Transformation

Patricia Washington's creative discovery illustrates how recognizing your divine DNA creates both quantifiable and unquantifiable returns.

Patricia was a 45-year-old social worker who'd been buying $25 worth of lottery tickets weekly for six years. She wasn't financially desperate, but she felt stuck in her career and frustrated by her inability to make a bigger impact in her community.

Patricia's transformation began when she attended a financial workshop at her church and calculated that she'd spent $7,800 on lottery tickets over six years. "I was devastated," she recalled. "I realized I could have funded a master's degree with that money."

Instead of regret, Patricia chose redirection:

Year 1: Used her lottery money to take online courses in community development and grant writing **Year 2**: Volunteered with local nonprofits to gain experience while continuing education **Year 3**: Launched a consulting practice helping small nonprofits write grants and develop programs

Results after three years:

- Patricia's consulting income exceeded her social work salary

- She'd helped twelve organizations secure over $200,000 in grant funding
- Her community impact had multiplied exponentially
- She'd developed expertise that made her valuable to organizations nationwide

"The lottery offered me a tiny chance at individual wealth," Patricia reflected. "Creative investment gave me a guaranteed chance at community wealth—the ability to create resources that benefit everyone, including me."

The Economic Impact of Creative Development

From a purely practical standpoint, developing your creative capacity is one of the best financial investments you can make. The Bureau of Labor Statistics reports that "creative economy" jobs—positions that require innovative thinking and problem-solving—are growing at twice the rate of traditional jobs and typically pay 30-50% more than routine positions.

But the economic benefits extend beyond employment. Creative people are more likely to:

- Start successful businesses
- Advance in their careers
- Develop multiple income streams
- Create intellectual property
- Build valuable professional networks

Consider these examples from people I've known personally:

Janet, a nurse who developed a more efficient patient charting system, received a $5,000 innovation bonus and was promoted to quality improvement coordinator with a $15,000 salary increase.

Robert, a maintenance worker who invented a simple tool to speed equipment repairs, patented his invention and now receives royalty payments that exceed his original salary.

Lisa, a teacher who created an innovative reading program, was hired as a curriculum consultant and now earns more in three months than she previously made in a year.

None of these people won the lottery. They discovered and developed their creative DNA, which provided sustainable financial benefits that continue growing over time.

The Creativity Multiplier Effect

One of the most powerful aspects of creative DNA is its multiplier effect. Unlike lottery winnings, which diminish with use, creative abilities grow stronger with exercise.

Dr. Mihaly Csikszentmihalyi's research on "flow states" reveals that people who regularly engage their creative abilities experience:

- Increased confidence in their problem-solving capacity

- Enhanced ability to see opportunities others miss
- Greater resilience during difficult circumstances
- Improved relationships through collaborative creativity
- Higher levels of life satisfaction and purpose

Moreover, creative solutions often address multiple problems simultaneously. When Michael Chen developed his computer therapy program, he didn't just help psychiatric patients—he also reduced staff turnover, decreased treatment costs, and created a model that other facilities could adopt.

PRACTICAL EXERCISE: The Creative Portfolio Building

Start building your creative portfolio immediately:

Month 1: Document Your Current Creative Assets

- List problems you've solved in the past year
- Identify systems you've improved
- Record positive feedback you've received about your ideas
- Note situations where you've helped others succeed

Month 2: Develop One Core Creative Skill

- Choose your strongest creative area from the assessment
- Invest your former lottery money in learning/improving this skill

- Practice this skill through volunteer projects or side opportunities
- Connect with others who share this creative interest

Month 3: Apply Your Creativity to Solve Real Problems

- Identify a problem in your workplace, community, or church
- Develop a creative solution using your enhanced skills
- Implement your solution and measure the results
- Share your success story to inspire others and build your reputation

The Stewardship Imperative

Here's a sobering thought: Your creative abilities are not your own property—they're gifts from God that you're called to steward for His purposes and others' benefit.

The parable of the talents (Matthew 25:14-30) isn't primarily about money—it's about stewarding whatever God has entrusted to us, including our creative capacity. The servant who buried his talent was condemned not for being evil, but for being passive. He failed to develop and multiply what he'd been given.

When you buy lottery tickets instead of developing your creativity, you're essentially burying your talent. You're saying,

"I don't believe the abilities God gave me are sufficient, so I'm hoping for external rescue instead of internal development."

But God expects us to multiply our talents, including our creative abilities. This multiplication serves multiple purposes:

- It glorifies God by reflecting His creative nature
- It serves others by solving problems and creating value
- It fulfills us by aligning our lives with our divine design
- It provides sustainable resources for kingdom work

> **YOUR MIRROR QUESTION** *What if you discovered that the creative abilities you've been dismissing as "not special" are actually God's provision system for your life? What if developing these gifts could provide better financial returns than any lottery? What would you do differently starting today?*

The DNA Test Results

After reading this chapter and potentially completing the 30-day challenge, you should have a clearer understanding of your creative DNA. Here's what the "test results" might reveal:

If you discovered analytical creativity: You solve problems through research, data analysis, and systematic thinking. Your superpower is seeing patterns others miss and developing logical solutions.

If you discovered relational creativity: You solve problems by bringing people together, building bridges, and creating harmony. Your superpower is helping others collaborate effectively.

If you discovered practical creativity: You solve problems by improving systems, processes, and procedures. Your superpower is making things work better, faster, or more efficiently.

If you discovered artistic creativity: You solve problems by helping people see beauty, meaning, and possibility. Your superpower is inspiring others through expression and imagination.

If you discovered entrepreneurial creativity: You solve problems by seeing opportunities, taking calculated risks, and creating value. Your superpower is turning ideas into reality.

If you discovered multiple forms: Congratulations—you're a creative hybrid with the ability to approach problems from multiple angles.

The Creative Covenant

As we conclude this chapter, I want to invite you to make a creative covenant—a commitment to steward your divine DNA responsibly:

"I acknowledge that I am made in the image of a creative God and therefore carry creative capacity within my DNA. I commit to discovering, developing, and deploying my creative abilities for God's glory and others' benefit. Instead of hoping for external rescue through lottery winnings, I will create internal solutions through the gifts God has given me. I will not bury my talents but will multiply them. I will not wait for luck but will create through faith. I recognize that my creativity is not my own possession but God's gift to be stewarded for His purposes."

The Ultimate Creative Act

The ultimate creative act isn't building a business, composing a masterpiece, or inventing a new technology—though these are all valuable. The ultimate creative act is becoming the person God designed you to be and helping others do the same.

When you discover and develop your creative DNA, you're not just solving practical problems. You're participating in God's ongoing creative work in the world. You're fulfilling your fundamental purpose as an image-bearer of the Creator.

The lottery promises to change your circumstances. Creativity promises to change you.

The lottery offers temporary windfall. Creativity offers permanent transformation.

The lottery might make you wealthy. Creativity makes you valuable.

Your divine DNA doesn't need a lottery win to activate. It just needs your willingness to discover and develop what God has already placed within you.

The creative gene is real. It's yours. It's time to let it express itself.

Next up: Chapter 10, where we'll explore the moment when God becomes enough—when you realize that divine relationship provides everything the lottery promises and more.

CHAPTER 10

When God Becomes Enough

"But godliness with contentment is great gain. For we brought nothing into the world, and we can take nothing out of it. But if we have food and clothing, we will be content with that." ---1 Timothy 6:6-8

Maybe you're not a 62-year-old minister, but you're the middle manager who finally stopped checking your investment accounts obsessively, who can look at your bank balance without that familiar knot of anxiety, who discovered that peace isn't a number—it's a Person.

Maybe you're not a healthcare worker, but you're the teacher who realized that contentment isn't about getting everything you want—it's about wanting what God has already given you, and finding that it's more than enough.

Maybe you've never sat at a kitchen table reading bank statements without panic, but you've had moments of profound peace when you realized that your security doesn't come from your circumstances—it comes from your relationship with the One who controls all circumstances.

If you've ever wondered what it would feel like to truly need nothing beyond what you already have in Christ, then you're ready for the most radical transformation possible: the moment when God becomes enough.

> **CULTURAL SPOTLIGHT: The Contentment Crisis** *Despite having access to more wealth, convenience, and opportunity than any generation in history, Americans report lower levels of life satisfaction than in the 1950s. The American Psychological Association found that 72% of Americans report money as a significant source of stress, while countries with lower average incomes often report higher happiness levels. Researchers call this "the contentment paradox"—the more we have, the less satisfied we become.*

Six months ago, Jennifer Walsh experienced what she now calls "the most liberating moment of my life."

Jennifer, a 34-year-old marketing coordinator and mother of two, had been playing the lottery faithfully for eight years. Not excessively—just $20 a week—but consistently. She had her system: family birthdays for Powerball, random Quick Picks for Mega Millions.

"I wasn't addicted," Jennifer explains. "I just always felt like I was one number away from solving all our problems. The mortgage, the kids' college funds, my husband's student loans—everything would be okay if I could just win."

The transformation came during an ordinary Tuesday morning when Jennifer's daughter asked a simple question that changed everything.

"Mommy," seven-year-old Emma said over breakfast, "why do you always seem worried about money when God takes care of everything?"

Jennifer paused, cereal spoon halfway to her mouth. Out of the mouths of babes.

"That afternoon, I sat in my car after buying what I didn't know would be my last lottery ticket," Jennifer continues. "Emma's question kept echoing: 'Why do you seem worried when God takes care of everything?' And I realized she was right. I'd been saying I trusted God while simultaneously preparing for the possibility that He wouldn't come through."

Jennifer threw the ticket away without checking the numbers. "Not because I felt guilty, but because I finally understood that I already had everything I needed. Not everything I wanted, but everything I needed. And for the first time in years, that felt like enough."

That was the moment God became enough for Jennifer Walsh.

> **KINGDOM PRINCIPLE** True contentment isn't the absence of desire—it's the presence of satisfaction in God's character regardless of circumstances. When God becomes enough, you don't stop wanting things to improve; you stop needing them to improve for you to be okay.

The Insufficiency Epidemic

We live in a culture of magnificent insufficiency. No matter how much we have, it's never quite enough. No matter how comfortable our circumstances, there's always something missing. No matter how blessed our lives, there's always a gap between what is and what we think should be.

Dr. Tim Kasser, a psychologist at Knox College who studies materialism and well-being, has documented what he calls "the hedonic treadmill"—the phenomenon where people quickly return to a baseline level of happiness despite positive or negative life changes.

"People think that getting more money, more possessions, or more status will make them significantly happier," Dr. Kasser explains. "But research consistently shows that after a brief spike, happiness levels return to where they were before. The problem isn't that people don't get what they want—it's that what they want keeps expanding."

This insufficiency epidemic explains the lottery industry's success. Lottery tickets aren't really about money—they're about the illusion that external additions can create internal satisfaction. But satisfaction isn't a math problem that can be solved by adding larger numbers. It's a spiritual problem that can only be resolved by discovering that God is enough.

The Story of David and Karen Mitchell

David and Karen Mitchell reached the place where God became enough through the most unlikely circumstances. I met them when David was a patient in our cardiac unit following his second heart attack at age 52.

For fifteen years, David had been chasing financial success with an intensity that was literally killing him. He worked seventy-hour weeks as a sales manager, invested aggressively in get-rich-quick schemes, and spent roughly $200 monthly on lottery tickets. Karen worked full-time as a bank teller while managing their household and raising their two teenagers.

"We were always just one break away from having enough," Karen told me during one of David's hospital stays. "David was convinced that if he could just close one big deal or win one lottery drawing, we could finally relax. But the goal kept moving. Every time we reached a financial milestone, David raised the bar higher."

David's second heart attack was the wake-up call that changed everything. Facing his mortality at 52, David began to question whether the life he was building was worth the life he was losing.

"I was lying in that hospital bed, probably going to survive but definitely going to live differently, when I realized I had been chasing the wrong thing," David reflected six months later. "I thought I needed more money to be happy. But what I actually needed was more peace. And peace wasn't for sale."

David and Karen made radical changes. David took early retirement with reduced benefits. They downsized their house, sold David's expensive car, and drastically simplified their lifestyle. Most importantly, they stopped buying lottery tickets and started investing that money in experiences rather than hopes.

"The weird thing," Karen observed a year later, "was that we were happier with less money than we'd ever been with more money. We had been so focused on what we didn't have that we'd missed what we did have: each other, our health, our family, our faith."

David lived nine more healthy years before passing peacefully in his sleep at 61. "Those nine years were the best years of our marriage," Karen told me at his funeral. "Because David finally learned that God was enough. And when God became enough for him, everything else became more than enough too."

> **LOTTERY FACT BOX** *Neuroscientist Dr. Alex Korb's research shows that people who practice gratitude and contentment have increased activity in the hypothalamus (which regulates stress), higher levels of dopamine, better sleep quality, improved immune function, and enhanced decision-making capacity. Gratitude literally rewires the brain for contentment.*

The Four Stages of God Becoming Enough

In my experience counseling people through financial anxiety and spiritual growth, I've observed four stages that people typically go through as God becomes sufficient in their lives:

Stage 1: Recognition This is when you first recognize that your restlessness, anxiety, and lottery-ticket buying are symptoms of spiritual insufficiency rather than material insufficiency. You begin to understand that no external addition will create internal satisfaction.

Stage 2: Reorientation This is when you begin to shift your focus from what you lack to what you have, from what you want God to give you to who God is. You start practicing gratitude, not as a technique to get more, but as recognition of what's already yours.

Stage 3: Relationship This is when your relationship with God deepens from transactional to relational. Instead of seeing God as a divine vending machine who should respond to your inputs with desired outputs, you begin to find satisfaction in God Himself regardless of what He provides.

Stage 4: Rest This is when contentment becomes your default setting rather than anxiety. You reach the place where God's presence, character, and promises are genuinely sufficient for peace, joy, and security regardless of circumstances.

> ***READER REFLECTION** Which stage best describes where you are currently? What would it take for you to move to the next stage? What specific fears or attachments might you need to release to let God become more sufficient in your life?*

The Practical Sufficiency Test

How do you know if God has become enough in your life? Here are some practical indicators:

Financial Peace Test

- You can look at your bank balance without anxiety
- You don't compulsively check investment accounts or lottery results
- You can be generous without worrying about having enough left
- You make financial decisions based on wisdom rather than fear

- You view money as a tool rather than a source of security

Circumstantial Contentment Test

- You can be genuinely happy for others' success without feeling diminished
- You don't constantly compare your life to others' highlight reels
- You find joy in ordinary moments rather than waiting for extraordinary events
- You're grateful for what you have rather than frustrated by what you lack
- You can worship God honestly even during difficult seasons

Relational Security Test

- You don't need others' approval to feel valuable
- You can love people without needing them to complete you
- You're comfortable being alone without feeling lonely
- You can serve others without expecting reciprocation
- You find your identity in God's love rather than others' opinions

Future Faith Test

- You can plan for the future without being anxious about it

- You trust God's provision even when you can't see how He'll provide
- You're content with God's timing rather than demanding your timeline
- You can take reasonable risks without being paralyzed by worst-case scenarios
- You view challenges as opportunities for growth rather than threats to your security

PRACTICAL EXERCISE: The Contentment Practices

If you want to reach the place where God becomes enough, here are practices that can help cultivate contentment:

Morning Gratitude Before checking your phone, stocks, or lottery results, list five things you're grateful for. Start with basics: health, family, shelter, faith, opportunities. This trains your brain to recognize abundance before seeking additions.

Evening Reflection Before bed, identify three ways you saw God's provision, protection, or presence during the day. This develops your ability to recognize God's sufficiency in ordinary circumstances.

Weekly Worship Spend time each week worshiping God for who He is rather than what He provides. Praise His character, faithfulness, wisdom, and love. This builds relationship rather than transaction.

Monthly Service Find ways to serve others who have less than you do. This provides perspective on your own abundance while participating in God's provision for others.

Annual Assessment Once a year, reflect on how God has been faithful over the past twelve months. Document answered prayers, unexpected provisions, personal growth, and relationship developments.

The Story of Margaret Williams's Breakthrough

Margaret Williams learned about true sufficiency through an experience that would have devastated most people but ended up being her gateway to contentment.

Margaret was a 68-year-old widow who came to our psychiatric unit after a severe depression following what she called "the worst year of my life." In twelve months, she'd lost her husband to cancer, her home to foreclosure, and her savings to medical bills. She was living in a studio apartment, working part-time at a grocery store, and struggling with anxiety about her future.

"I keep thinking that if I could just win something—the lottery, a sweepstakes, anything—I could get my life back," Margaret told me during our initial session. "I spend twenty dollars a week on tickets because I don't know what else to do."

Over the six weeks Margaret was in our care, something remarkable happened. Through grief counseling, spiritual direction, and group therapy, Margaret began to rediscover resources she'd forgotten she had.

"I started making a gratitude list every morning," she explained during one of our sessions. "At first, I could barely find three things. But as the weeks went on, the list got longer. I realized I wasn't as poor as I thought I was."

Margaret's list included things like:

- Her grandson who called every Sunday
- Her ability to make soup that helped her neighbors feel better
- Her knowledge of bargain shopping that could help other seniors
- Her strong faith that had carried her through previous difficulties
- Her gentle spirit that brought peace to anxious people

Six weeks after admission, Margaret's perspective had completely transformed. Not because her circumstances had improved—she was still living in the studio apartment, still working at the grocery store—but because she'd discovered that God's presence in her reduced circumstances was sufficient for joy, purpose, and peace.

"I stopped buying lottery tickets three weeks ago," Margaret told me during her discharge meeting. "Not because I felt guilty about it, but because I realized I didn't need to win anything. I had already won everything that mattered. I just hadn't been looking in the right place."

The Mathematics of Enough

The world operates on addition mathematics: Happiness equals what you have plus what you get. This equation creates an endless cycle of insufficiency because no finite addition can satisfy infinite desire.

God operates on multiplication mathematics: Contentment equals what you have times your gratitude for it. In this equation, even small blessings become substantial when multiplied by appreciation, and substantial blessings become overwhelming when multiplied by worship.

Consider Jesus feeding the 5,000 (Matthew 14:13-21). The disciples saw the math problem: Five loaves plus two fish plus 5,000 people equals insufficiency. Jesus saw multiplication potential: Five loaves times faith equals abundance for everyone with leftovers remaining.

The miracle wasn't that Jesus created food from nothing. The miracle was that He multiplied what was already available. And He's still doing the same thing today—multiplying what you already have when you offer it to Him with faith.

The Paradox of Enough

Here's the beautiful paradox of contentment: When you reach the place where God is enough, He often provides more than enough materially as well. Not because contentment is a technique for getting more, but because contentment creates the character and wisdom needed to steward abundance responsibly.

Dr. Robert Emmons, a gratitude researcher at UC Davis, has found that grateful people typically earn higher incomes, save more money, and make better financial decisions than their less grateful counterparts. They're also more generous, which creates positive social and economic networks that lead to additional opportunities.

"Contentment isn't the enemy of prosperity," Dr. Emmons explains. "It's actually prosperity's best friend because it creates the internal stability needed to make wise external choices."

PRACTICAL EXERCISE: The Enough Declaration

As this chapter concludes, I want to invite you to make an "enough declaration"—a statement of faith that God's presence, provision, and promises are sufficient for every need, every dream, every fear, and every hope:

"I declare that God is enough. Not because my circumstances are perfect, but because His character is perfect. Not because I have everything I want, but because I have everything I need in Him. Not because my problems have disappeared, but because my Problem-Solver never leaves. I choose contentment over complaint, gratitude over greed, trust over anxiety. I will not let insufficient feelings override God's sufficient promises. He is enough. He has always been enough. And in Him, I am more than enough."

The Liberation of Limits

One of the most liberating discoveries in the journey toward contentment is that limits aren't limitations—they're liberations. When you accept that you don't need unlimited resources to live a rich life, you're free to enjoy the resources you have.

This liberation affects every area of life:

- **Time:** Instead of wishing you had more hours, you learn to savor the hours you have
- **Money:** Instead of needing more income, you learn to live richly within your income
- **Relationships:** Instead of seeking perfect people, you learn to love imperfect people perfectly
- **Circumstances:** Instead of demanding ideal situations, you learn to find God in real situations

- **Future:** Instead of controlling outcomes, you learn to trust the Outcome-Controller

When Worship Replaces Worry

The ultimate sign that God has become enough is when worship replaces worry as your default response to challenges. Instead of immediately calculating how you'll solve problems, you first acknowledge that God is bigger than any problem you'll face.

This doesn't mean you become passive or irresponsible. It means you approach challenges from a position of faith rather than fear, abundance rather than scarcity, trust rather than control.

When your car breaks down, your first thought is, "God will provide" rather than "How will I afford this?"

When your job is threatened, your first response is prayer rather than panic.

When your health is challenged, your first instinct is to trust God's sovereignty rather than despair about the future.

This shift from worry to worship is the practical evidence that God has become sufficient for every area of your life.

> **YOUR MIRROR QUESTION** *What would your life look like if you truly believed that God's love for you, His presence with you, and His promises to you were sufficient for complete peace and joy? What would you do differently? What would you stop trying to control? What contentment would you experience?*

The Ripple Effect of Contentment

When God becomes enough for you, it creates a ripple effect that impacts everyone around you:

- **Your family** experiences peace instead of anxiety, security instead of stress
- **Your coworkers** see an example of someone who isn't driven by desperation or greed
- **Your church** benefits from someone who serves out of gratitude rather than guilt
- **Your community** gains a person who contributes rather than just consumes
- **Your legacy** becomes one of faith rather than fear, trust rather than worry

Contentment is contagious. When people see someone living with genuine peace and satisfaction, it gives them permission to stop chasing what they thought they needed and start appreciating what they already have.

The Sacred Sufficiency

The moment when God becomes enough isn't the end of desire—it's the beginning of desire fulfilled. When you stop needing God to be more than He is, you discover that He's already more than you imagined.

When you stop needing more from life, you discover that life already contains more than you recognized.

When you stop waiting for enough to come from outside, you realize that enough was inside all along.

The lottery promises that enough is just six numbers away. God promises that enough is just one prayer away.

The lottery suggests that enough requires luck. God guarantees that enough requires faith.

The lottery says enough comes from getting. God says enough comes from receiving what you've already been given.

Stop playing the lottery of insufficiency. Start living the reality of divine sufficiency.

God is enough. He has always been enough. And with Him, you have more than enough.

Next up: Chapter 11, where we'll explore the practical steps for making the great exchange—trading lottery dreams for kingdom reality and building wealth God's way.

CHAPTER 11

The Great Exchange: Trading Lottery Dreams for Kingdom Reality

"Do not store up for yourselves treasures on earth, where moths and vermin destroy, and where thieves break in and steal. But store up for yourselves treasures in heaven, where moths and vermin do not destroy, and where thieves do not break in and steal." ---Matthew 6:19-20

Maybe you're not a ministry leader, but you're the accountant who finally stopped at the gas station this morning, looked at the lottery display, and walked away—not because you felt guilty, but because you finally understood that you already possess everything you need to create the abundance you've been hoping to win.

Maybe you're not a nurse, but you're the parent who realized that the $50 you've been spending monthly on scratch-offs could fund your child's music lessons, your own online course, or a dozen other investments that compound rather than disappear.

Maybe you've never thrown a lottery ticket in a kitchen trash can, but you've had a moment when you decided to stop waiting for external rescue and start creating internal solutions—the moment you chose to become the answer to your own prayers.

If you've ever wondered what it would look like to completely redirect your hope from random chance to purposeful choice, then you're ready for the great exchange: trading lottery dreams for kingdom reality.

> **CULTURAL SPOTLIGHT: The Investment Difference**
> *Financial advisor Dave Ramsey tracked 10,000 millionaires and found that 79% built wealth gradually through consistent investing, skill development, and business building—never through gambling or lottery wins. Meanwhile, lottery players who spend $50 monthly for 30 years ($18,000 total) typically accumulate zero wealth, while investors who put that same $50 monthly into index funds average $175,000 over the same period. The great exchange isn't just spiritual—it's mathematical.*

Last Tuesday morning, Sarah Chen made the great exchange in the most ordinary way imaginable.

Sarah, a 29-year-old dental assistant and mother of two, had been buying lottery tickets every Tuesday for six years—always the same $15 worth, always the same gas station on her way to work. It had become as routine as getting coffee.

But this Tuesday was different. As Sarah walked toward the lottery counter, she noticed a flyer for community college courses. One particular class caught her eye: "Dental Hygiene Certification—Evening Program."

For five minutes, Sarah stood between the lottery counter and the information rack, holding the flyer. Finally, she did something that surprised her: Instead of buying tickets, she took the flyer home.

"That night, I calculated what I'd been spending on lottery tickets," Sarah recalls. "Six years, fifty-two weeks a year, fifteen dollars a week. It was $4,680. I had literally played away a year's tuition for the certification that could double my income."

Within a week, Sarah had enrolled in the dental hygiene program. She used her Tuesday lottery money for textbooks and study materials. Eighteen months later, she graduated and immediately received job offers starting at $32 per hour—a 60% increase from her previous salary.

"I spent six years hoping random numbers would change my life," Sarah reflects. "But the real change happened when I invested those same dollars in myself. I traded lottery dreams for education reality, and the return was guaranteed."

Sarah's story illustrates the power of the great exchange—the moment when you stop hoping for external intervention and start creating internal transformation.

> **KINGDOM PRINCIPLE** *The great exchange isn't just about stopping one behavior and starting another—it's about fundamentally shifting from passive hope to active faith, from external dependence to internal development, from consumer mindset to creator mindset. You stop waiting for provision and start becoming provision.*

The Psychology of Exchange

Dr. Daniel Kahneman, the Nobel Prize-winning psychologist, has studied what he calls "loss aversion"—the human tendency to feel the pain of losing something more intensely than the pleasure of gaining something equivalent. This psychological principle explains why the great exchange feels difficult initially.

When you stop buying lottery tickets, your brain doesn't just register the logical benefits—it mourns the loss of possibility, however remote. You're not just giving up pieces of paper; you're giving up dreams, fantasies, and the comfort of believing that rescue might come from outside.

But here's what Dr. Kahneman's research also reveals: Once people successfully make a beneficial exchange and experience its results, the new pattern becomes more psychologically rewarding than the old one. The key is surviving the transition period when you feel the loss but haven't yet experienced the gain.

"The most successful behavioral changes," Dr. Kahneman explains, "involve replacing one reward system with a more satisfying reward system, not just eliminating rewards altogether."

The great exchange works because you're not eliminating the dream of abundance—you're replacing lottery abundance with kingdom abundance. You're not giving up hope for a better life—you're choosing a better path to that life.

The Three-Part Exchange

The great exchange involves three simultaneous transitions that work together to create lasting transformation:

Part 1: From Passive Hope to Active Faith

- **Old Pattern:** Buying tickets and hoping external forces will rescue you
- **New Pattern:** Using your God-given abilities to create solutions and trusting God to multiply your efforts

Part 2: From Instant Gratification to Compound Growth

- **Old Pattern:** Seeking immediate windfall that solves all problems at once
- **New Pattern:** Making small, consistent investments in character, skills, and relationships that compound over time

Part 3: From Individual Gain to Kingdom Impact

- **Old Pattern:** Hoping to accumulate resources for personal benefit
- **New Pattern:** Developing abilities to create value that benefits others while providing for yourself

> **LOTTERY FACT BOX** *Behavioral economists have found that people who make "replacement investments" (using gambling money for education, skills, or business development) show 89% success rates in maintaining the new behavior, compared to only 23% success rates for people who simply try to stop gambling without redirecting the money toward something meaningful.*

The Story of Carlos Ramirez's Transformation

Let me tell you about Carlos Ramirez, a maintenance supervisor who made the great exchange in the most practical way imaginable.

Carlos had been buying lottery tickets for twelve years, spending roughly sixty dollars monthly on various games. He wasn't addicted in any clinical sense, but the tickets had become his primary financial hope. "I figured it was my only shot at getting ahead," Carlos told me. "I don't have a college degree, don't have family money, don't have any special skills. The lottery was my retirement plan."

Carlos's transformation began when his daughter Maria started asking questions about his lottery habit during her high school economics class. "She had to do a project on probability and statistics," Carlos recalled. "She calculated that I had spent over $8,000 on lottery tickets in twelve years and won back maybe $300. She asked me what else I could have done with that money."

The Great Exchange: Trading Lottery Dreams for Kingdom Reality

That question led Carlos to make his great exchange, but he did it gradually rather than abruptly:

Month 1-2: Instead of buying lottery tickets, Carlos put the sixty dollars into a savings account. "It felt weird at first," he admitted. "I kept wanting to check lottery results even though I hadn't played."

Month 3-4: Carlos used his monthly sixty dollars to take an online course in HVAC repair. "I figured if I was going to gamble, I'd gamble on myself instead of random numbers."

Month 5-6: Carlos started doing small HVAC jobs for friends and neighbors on weekends, charging modest fees and building a reputation for reliable work.

Month 7-12: Word spread about Carlos's skills and reasonable prices. He was earning an extra $200-400 monthly from side jobs, far more than he'd ever won from lottery tickets.

Year 2: Carlos launched his own HVAC business while keeping his hospital job. His lottery replacement fund had grown to $1,440—more than he'd won in twelve years of playing.

Year 3: Carlos's business was generating enough income for him to reduce his hospital hours while maintaining the same total income.

"The lottery promised to make me rich overnight," Carlos reflected three years after his exchange. "But investing in myself made me rich over time, and it also made me proud of what I'd built. I realized that I'd been spending money hoping to become lucky when I should have been spending money becoming skilled."

> **READER REFLECTION** *Calculate what you've spent on lottery tickets, gambling, or get-rich-quick schemes in the past year. Now imagine investing that same amount in education, skill development, or business building. What transformation could you fund with money you've been spending on hope? What would change if you invested in yourself instead of chance?*

The 90-Day Exchange Program

If you're ready to make the great exchange but aren't sure how to begin, here's a practical 90-day program that has helped hundreds of people transition from lottery dreams to kingdom reality:

Days 1-30: Foundation Phase

Week 1: Calculate the Cost

- Add up everything you've spent on lottery tickets, scratch-offs, and other gambling in the past year
- Research what that amount could have purchased: education, tools, equipment, or experiences

- Set up a "Kingdom Investment Fund" account and commit to depositing your lottery money there instead

Week 2: Identify Your Investment Area

- Complete a skills assessment: What abilities do you have that could be developed?
- Consider character areas where you want to grow: patience, wisdom, leadership, communication
- Identify service opportunities that align with your interests and abilities

Week 3: Create Your Investment Plan

- Choose one skill to develop over the next 90 days
- Select one character quality to focus on through prayer, study, and practice
- Find one way to serve others that requires some of your lottery money as investment

Week 4: Begin Implementation

- Start your chosen skill development program
- Begin daily practices to develop your chosen character quality
- Make your first service investment, however small

Days 31-60: Development Phase

Week 5-6: Skill Building

- Continue your skill development with consistent daily practice
- Document your progress and celebrate small improvements
- Connect with others who share your learning goals

Week 7-8: Character Growth

- Deepen your spiritual disciplines related to your chosen character quality
- Seek opportunities to practice this quality in real-life situations
- Ask trusted friends to provide feedback on your growth

Days 61-90: Application Phase

Week 9-10: Integration

- Begin using your developing skills in practical ways
- Look for opportunities to demonstrate your growing character qualities
- Increase your service investment as your confidence grows

Week 11-12: Multiplication

- Share what you're learning with others
- Look for ways to use your skills to serve or earn
- Evaluate your progress and plan your next 90-day cycle

The Story of Janet and Robert Turner

Janet and Robert Turner made their great exchange as a couple, which created even more powerful results than individual transformation.

For eight years, Janet and Robert had been spending $150 monthly on lottery tickets—$75 each from their individual "fun money" budgets. They weren't struggling financially, but they weren't getting ahead either, and both felt frustrated by their lack of progress toward retirement goals.

Their exchange began when Robert's work offered tuition reimbursement for business courses and Janet found a community college program in nonprofit management that had always interested her.

"We realized we were spending $1,800 per year hoping to get rich," Janet explained, "when we could spend that same money getting educated, which was practically guaranteed to improve our income."

Their great exchange involved coordinating their individual investments:

Robert's Investment: Used his $75 monthly to pay for business courses in project management and leadership **Janet's Investment**: Used her $75 monthly for nonprofit management classes and volunteer leadership training **Joint Investment**: Combined their lottery money during alternate months to fund shared experiences: marriage retreats, financial planning workshops, and ministry training

The results exceeded their expectations:

Year 1: Robert's project management certification led to a promotion with a $8,000 salary increase **Year 2:** Janet's nonprofit training helped her launch a consulting business serving small ministries **Year 3:** Their combined income had increased by $18,000 annually, and they'd developed skills that continued growing in value

"The lottery would have given us money without changing us," Robert reflected. "Education gave us the ability to create money while becoming better people. We traded hoping for a windfall for building wind power—the internal capacity to generate income consistently."

PRACTICAL EXERCISE: The Kingdom Investment Calculator

Step 1: Calculate Your Lottery/Gambling Expenses

- Weekly lottery tickets: $____
- Monthly scratch-offs: $____
- Annual casino visits: $____
- Online gambling: $____
- **Total Annual Gambling Expense: $____**

Step 2: Calculate Potential Kingdom Investments With your annual gambling expense, you could:

- Take ____ college courses at $150 each
- Buy ____ books for personal development at $15 each
- Fund ____ hours of professional coaching at $50/hour
- Support ____ missionaries at $50/month each
- Provide ____ meals for homeless individuals at $5 each

Step 3: Project 10-Year Kingdom ROI If you invested your gambling money in skills development:

- Year 1: New skills acquired
- Year 3: Increased income potential
- Year 5: Enhanced career opportunities
- Year 10: Compounded benefits to yourself and others

Building Wealth God's Way

The great exchange isn't just about stopping lottery purchases—it's about learning to build wealth according to kingdom principles. God's wealth-building system is fundamentally different from both lottery thinking and conventional get-rich-quick schemes.

Kingdom Wealth-Building Principles:

Gradual Rather Than Sudden Proverbs 13:11 teaches, "Dishonest money dwindles away, but whoever gathers money little by little makes it grow." Kingdom wealth builds slowly but sustainably.

Service Rather Than Self-Focus Matthew 20:26-27 promises, "Whoever wants to become great among you must be your servant, and whoever wants to be first must be slave of all." Kingdom wealth comes through creating value for others.

Character Rather Than Cleverness Proverbs 22:1 declares, "A good name is more desirable than great riches; to be esteemed is better than silver or gold." Kingdom wealth prioritizes integrity over income.

Generosity Rather Than Accumulation Luke 6:38 assures, "Give, and it will be given to you. A good measure, pressed down, shaken together and running over, will be poured into your lap." Kingdom wealth flows toward generous people.

Faith Rather Than Fear Philippians 4:19 promises, "And my God will meet all your needs according to the riches of his glory in Christ Jesus." Kingdom wealth operates through trust rather than anxiety.

The Practical Tools for Exchange

Making the great exchange requires practical tools that help you redirect lottery energy toward kingdom investments. Here are the most effective tools I've seen people use:

The Replacement Fund Open a separate savings account designated specifically for kingdom investments. Every time you would have bought a lottery ticket, deposit that money instead. Watch it grow from something that would have disappeared into something that compounds.

The Skills Ladder Identify a progression of skills you want to develop over the next five years. Start with foundation skills, then intermediate, then advanced. Each skill you master becomes a rung on the ladder toward greater capability and earning potential.

The Service Portfolio Develop multiple ways to serve others using your time, talents, and treasure. Like a financial portfolio, a service portfolio spreads risk and increases opportunities for unexpected returns.

The Character Journal Track your growth in specific character qualities through daily reflection. Record situations where you practiced patience, demonstrated integrity, or showed wisdom. Character development is the foundation of all other kingdom investments.

The Kingdom Network Build relationships with others who are also committed to kingdom wealth-building. These relationships provide accountability, encouragement, and opportunities for collaboration.

PRACTICAL EXERCISE: Overcoming Exchange Resistance

Making the great exchange isn't always easy. Here are common forms of resistance and how to overcome them:

"What if I Miss the Big Win?"

- **Resistance:** Fear that you'll stop playing just before your numbers come up
- **Reality:** Your chances of winning remain virtually zero whether you play once or for decades
- **Response:** Remind yourself that you're trading a 1-in-300-million chance at lottery wealth for a 100% chance at character wealth

"My Problems Need Immediate Solutions"

- **Resistance:** Belief that your circumstances require instant rather than gradual improvement
- **Reality:** Most problems that feel urgent are actually chronic and require sustainable solutions
- **Response:** Focus on small, immediate improvements while building long-term capacity

"I Don't Have Any Marketable Skills"

- **Resistance:** Belief that you lack abilities worth developing
- **Reality:** Everyone has transferable skills and capacity for growth

- **Response:** Complete a thorough skills inventory with help from others who know you well

"Kingdom Investment Takes Too Long"

- **Resistance:** Impatience with gradual progress versus instant transformation
- **Reality:** Sustainable change requires time, and shortcuts usually lead to setbacks
- **Response:** Set short-term milestones that provide encouragement during long-term development

The Story of Patricia Washington's Legacy

Patricia Washington's great exchange illustrates how kingdom investment creates both immediate and generational impact.

Patricia was a 45-year-old social worker who'd been buying $25 worth of lottery tickets weekly for six years. Instead of continuing to hope for random rescue, Patricia made her great exchange:

Year 1: Used her lottery money to take online courses in community development and grant writing **Year 2:** Volunteered with local nonprofits to gain experience while continuing education **Year 3:** Launched a consulting practice helping small nonprofits write grants and develop programs

Results after five years:

- Patricia's consulting income exceeded her social work salary
- She'd helped twenty-three organizations secure over $450,000 in grant funding
- Her community impact had multiplied exponentially
- She'd developed expertise that made her valuable nationwide
- She was training other social workers in grant writing, multiplying her impact

"The lottery offered me a tiny chance at individual wealth," Patricia reflected. "Kingdom investment gave me a guaranteed chance at community wealth—the ability to create resources that benefit everyone, including me."

But the real transformation became apparent when Patricia's teenage daughter announced her college plans: "Mom, I want to study nonprofit management like you did. I want to help communities the way you do."

Patricia's kingdom investment had created a generational legacy that no lottery jackpot could match.

> **YOUR MIRROR QUESTION** *If you made the great exchange today—redirecting all your lottery spending toward kingdom investment—what would your life look like in five years? What skills would you have developed? What impact would you have made? What legacy would you be building? What's keeping you from starting that transformation today?*

The Exchange Commitment

As this chapter concludes, you face a choice: Will you continue hoping for lottery rescue, or will you commit to kingdom investment?

If you're ready to make the great exchange, consider signing this commitment:

"I commit to trading lottery dreams for kingdom reality. Instead of spending money on random chance, I will invest in my character, skills, and service capacity. Instead of hoping for external rescue, I will develop internal resources. Instead of seeking individual wealth, I will create value that benefits others while providing for my needs. I trust that God's system of gradual, sustainable, service-oriented wealth-building is superior to any lottery system. I will be patient with the process, faithful with small investments, and grateful for compound returns. This is my great exchange."

The Investment That Never Loses

The beautiful truth about kingdom investment is that it never truly loses value. Even when external circumstances are difficult, character development continues. Even when income fluctuates, skills remain. Even when opportunities seem scarce, service creates new possibilities.

The lottery promises a jackpot you probably won't win. Kingdom investment promises returns you definitely will win.

The lottery offers money that might be stolen, lost, or squandered. Kingdom investment offers wealth that can't be taken away.

The lottery provides temporary resources. Kingdom investment builds eternal capacity.

Make the great exchange. Trade lottery dreams for kingdom reality. Trade external dependence for internal confidence. Trade random hope for reliable investment.

Your kingdom portfolio is waiting. And unlike the lottery, everyone who invests wins.

Final chapter ahead: Chapter 12, where we'll discover why faith is the only bet where everyone can win, and issue the ultimate challenge to bet on forever rather than chance.

CHAPTER 12

Betting on Forever: The Only Guaranteed Win

"For what is a man profited, if he shall gain the whole world, and lose his own soul? Or what shall a man give in exchange for his soul?" --- Matthew 16:26

Maybe you're not a 60-year-old minister receiving a wooden box from his wife, but you're the office worker who just realized that your greatest treasures aren't in your investment account—they're in the relationships, memories, and character you've built over decades of faithful living.

Maybe you're not a healthcare professional, but you're the parent who finally understands that winning the lottery of love, purpose, and eternal security is infinitely more valuable than winning any Powerball drawing.

Maybe you've never counted medications at 3 AM, but you've had moments when you recognized that the most important bet you'll ever make isn't about six numbers—it's about forever, and the God who holds both time and eternity in His hands.

If you've ever wondered what it would mean to place your ultimate bet on something that absolutely, positively, guaranteed cannot lose, then you're ready for the final decision: betting on forever.

> **CULTURAL SPOTLIGHT: The Infinity Investment**
> *Mathematician Blaise Pascal famously argued that belief in God is the ultimate rational choice: "If God exists and you believe, you gain everything. If God exists and you don't believe, you lose everything. If God doesn't exist, believing costs you little while providing meaning and peace." Modern game theory confirms Pascal's logic—when the potential gain is infinite (eternal life), even a small probability of God's existence makes faith the only rational "bet."*

This morning, I sat in the same kitchen where I used to hide lottery tickets, reading a letter that changed how I think about winning forever.

The letter came from Marcus, a former patient I'd cared for during his gambling recovery three years ago. Marcus had lost his house, his marriage, and nearly his life to lottery addiction before finding his way to our psychiatric unit. When he left, he'd made a commitment to "bet on forever instead of chance."

"Dear Pastor," Marcus wrote, "I wanted to update you on how my 'forever bet' is going. Three years ago, I was spending $300 a week on lottery tickets and had lost everything that mattered. Today, I'm remarried to a woman who loves God, managing a crew of construction workers, and teaching a financial recovery class at our church.

"But here's what I really wanted to tell you: Last week, my stepson asked me what the best investment I'd ever made was. I could have talked about our house, or my business, or my savings account. Instead, I told him about the day I decided to bet everything on Jesus Christ.

"That single decision has paid dividends every day for three years: peace instead of anxiety, relationships instead of isolation, purpose instead of emptiness, hope instead of desperation. And the best part? The returns keep growing, and they'll continue forever.

"I used to think I needed to win the lottery to have abundant life. Now I know I already won the only lottery that matters. Thank you for helping me understand that betting on forever is the only bet where everyone wins."

Marcus had discovered what I pray you'll discover through this book: The ultimate jackpot isn't something you win—it's someone you already are, and Someone who already loves you.

KINGDOM PRINCIPLE *Betting on forever isn't gambling—it's the safest investment in the universe. While lottery tickets offer infinitesimal chances of temporary wealth, faith offers guaranteed chances of eternal wealth. The mathematics of eternity make this the only rational choice.*

The Eternal Perspective

The fundamental problem with lottery thinking isn't just that the odds are terrible (though they are) or that it wastes money (though it does). The fundamental problem is that it trains us to think in temporal rather than eternal terms.

The lottery asks: "What do you want to win right now?" Faith asks: "What do you want to win forever?"

The lottery focuses on immediate gratification that may or may not come. Faith focuses on eternal satisfaction that definitely will come.

The lottery promises rewards you can spend in this life. Faith promises rewards you can enjoy in the next life and beyond.

When you shift from temporal to eternal perspective, everything changes. Suddenly, the most important investments aren't in your 401(k) or your lottery numbers—they're in your character, your relationships, your service to others, and your relationship with God.

The Mathematics of Eternity

Dr. William Lane Craig, a philosopher and mathematician, has calculated what he calls "the eternal multiplication factor." His premise is simple: If life after death is eternal, then any investment that pays dividends beyond physical death has infinite return potential.

"Even if the probability of eternal life were only 50%," Dr. Craig explains, "the expected value of investing in eternity would still exceed any finite investment, no matter how large. You're essentially multiplying by infinity."

This isn't just theological speculation—it's mathematical reality. When you invest in things that last beyond this life, you're not just improving your current circumstances. You're participating in compound growth that continues forever.

Consider the eternal multiplication factor for different types of investments:

- **Lottery Tickets**: Return on investment ends at death (if you win at all)
- **Financial Investments**: Return on investment ends at death or when inheritance is spent
- **Character Development**: Returns continue into eternity through your transformed soul
- **Relationships**: Returns continue through eternal fellowship with loved ones
- **Service to Others**: Returns continue through the eternal impact of lives you've touched
- **Faith in God**: Returns continue through eternal relationship with your Creator

The mathematics are clear: Betting on forever always produces superior returns to betting on now.

> **LOTTERY FACT BOX** *According to the Bureau of Labor Statistics, Americans spend more money annually on lottery tickets ($95 billion) than on retirement savings ($74 billion). We're literally investing more in temporary fantasies than eternal realities, betting more on impossible odds than guaranteed futures.*

The Story of Harold Fletcher's Legacy

Let me tell you about Harold Fletcher, a janitor I met during my early nursing years who understood eternal mathematics better than any financial advisor I've ever known.

Harold worked the night shift at our hospital for thirty-seven years, making barely enough to support his family of five. He never owned a house, never drove a new car, never took expensive vacations. By worldly standards, Harold was unsuccessful. By eternal standards, Harold was wealthy beyond measure.

Every night as Harold cleaned the hospital floors, he prayed for the patients in each room. He left encouraging notes for struggling nurses. He used his modest salary to buy small gifts for patients who had no visitors. He mentored young employees who reminded him of his own children.

When Harold retired, the hospital held a celebration that packed the main conference room. Dozens of former patients attended to thank him for kindness they still remembered years later. Nurses shared stories of how his encouragement had kept them in healthcare during difficult seasons. Administrators testified about Harold's integrity and work ethic.

But the most remarkable testimony came from Harold's own children. All five had become successful professionals: two doctors, a teacher, an engineer, and a pastor. When asked about their success, they all credited their father's example of finding purpose in service rather than profit.

"Dad never won the lottery," Harold's oldest son told the gathering, "but he taught us something better: how to live a life so rich in love and service that every day feels like a jackpot."

Harold died two years after retirement, leaving behind no financial inheritance but an eternal legacy that continues to impact lives decades later. He had bet on forever and won in ways that lottery tickets could never match.

The Guaranteed Win Strategy

Unlike the lottery, which offers no guaranteed wins, betting on forever offers multiple guaranteed returns. Here are the guaranteed wins available to anyone who chooses eternal investment over temporal gambling:

Guaranteed Win #1: Character Transformation When you invest in spiritual growth, moral development, and wisdom acquisition, you're guaranteed to become a better person. This transformation may be gradual, but it's certain. Every prayer deepens your relationship with God. Every act of service develops your compassion. Every choice to forgive expands your capacity for love.

Guaranteed Win #2: Meaningful Relationships When you invest in authentic relationships rather than hoping for instant wealth, you're guaranteed to experience the richness of human connection. Love, friendship, and community provide satisfaction that money cannot purchase and security that lottery winnings cannot provide.

Guaranteed Win #3: Purpose and Significance When you invest your time and energy in serving others and advancing God's kingdom, you're guaranteed to experience purpose that transcends circumstances. This sense of significance doesn't depend on external validation or financial reward—it flows from knowing you're part of something bigger than yourself.

Guaranteed Win #4: Peace and Contentment When you trust God's provision rather than random chance, you're guaranteed to experience peace that surpasses understanding. This peace doesn't depend on perfect circumstances—it rests on perfect faith in an imperfect world.

Guaranteed Win #5: Eternal Security When you place your faith in Christ rather than lottery numbers, you're guaranteed eternal life and security that nothing can destroy.

This is the ultimate insurance policy that covers not just this life but all of existence.

> **READER REFLECTION** If you could choose between a guaranteed $100 million lottery win that comes with the statistical likelihood of relationship destruction, anxiety, and life problems, or guaranteed eternal life, perfect peace, unshakeable joy, and infinite love—which would you honestly choose? What does your answer reveal about what you really value?

The Story of Mary Chen's Compound Returns

Mary Chen's life illustrates the power of compound eternal investment.

I met Mary when she was 78 years old, hospitalized for a hip replacement. Despite her pain and the stress of surgery, Mary was the most joyful patient on our ward.

Mary had immigrated to America from Taiwan in 1962 with her husband and two young children. They arrived with $73, no English skills, and no job prospects. For the first five years, Mary worked as a seamstress while her husband washed dishes, both sending every spare dollar to English classes and their children's education.

"We could have spent money on lottery tickets like some of our friends," Mary told me during one of our conversations. "But we decided to bet on education instead. We figured the best jackpot would be raising children who could create their own opportunities."

Mary and her husband never became wealthy in conventional terms. But their eternal investment strategy produced remarkable returns:

Investment in Education: Both children became doctors and funded full scholarships for other immigrant students **Investment in Community:** Mary started an ESL program at her church that has helped over 500 immigrants learn English **Investment in Character:** Mary's reputation for integrity opened business opportunities that provided comfortable retirement **Investment in Faith:** Mary's trust in God during difficult times inspired dozens of people to deepen their own faith **Investment in Service:** Mary's volunteer work at a free clinic has provided medical care for thousands of uninsured patients

At 78, Mary's "portfolio" included two successful children, four grandchildren in college, a thriving community program, a legacy of service, and dozens of people whose lives were changed by her example.

"I never won the lottery," Mary smiled as I prepared her discharge paperwork. "But I won something better: a life so full of love and purpose that every day feels like a prize. That's what happens when you bet on forever instead of chance."

PRACTICAL EXERCISE: The Forever Portfolio

If you're going to bet on forever, you need a portfolio that transcends time. Here's how to build an eternal investment portfolio that guarantees returns:

Spiritual Assets

- **Prayer Life:** Regular communication with God that deepens relationship and provides guidance
- **Scripture Study:** Investment in wisdom and truth that transforms thinking and decision-making
- **Worship:** Practice of acknowledging God's worth that creates proper perspective on everything else
- **Fellowship:** Participation in faith community that provides support and accountability

Character Assets

- **Integrity:** Consistency between beliefs and actions that builds trust and opens opportunities
- **Compassion:** Ability to care for others that creates meaningful relationships and service opportunities
- **Wisdom:** Practical understanding that improves decision-making and problem-solving
- **Perseverance:** Capacity to continue during difficulty that builds strength and character

Relational Assets

- **Marriage**: Investment in lifelong partnership that provides companionship and stability
- **Family**: Commitment to raising and nurturing children who carry values into future generations
- **Friendship**: Development of genuine connections that provide mutual support and encouragement
- **Community**: Participation in groups that work together for common good

Service Assets

- **Ministry**: Use of gifts and abilities to serve God's purposes and advance His kingdom
- **Career**: Application of skills and talents in ways that benefit others while providing for family
- **Volunteerism**: Generous sharing of time and energy to address community needs
- **Mentoring**: Investment in others' development that multiplies impact across generations

Legacy Assets

- **Reputation**: Pattern of choices that creates lasting positive impression on others
- **Influence**: Platform for encouraging others to make faith-based rather than chance-based decisions
- **Wisdom**: Life lessons that can be passed on to help others avoid mistakes and embrace truth

- **Faith:** Model of trusting God that inspires others to do the same

The Compound Interest of Eternity

One of the most powerful aspects of betting on forever is the compound interest effect. Unlike lottery winnings that diminish over time, eternal investments grow exponentially as they accumulate benefits in this life and the next.

Consider how eternal investments compound:

Year 1: You develop habits of prayer, service, and character development **Year 5:** These habits have created patterns of peace, purpose, and positive relationships **Year 10:** The patterns have produced reputation, opportunities, and deep satisfaction **Year 25:** Your life has become a model that influences others to make similar investments **Year 50:** Your legacy extends through multiple generations and hundreds of relationships **Eternity:** Your investments continue producing returns forever through transformed lives and kingdom impact

This compounding effect explains why older believers often radiate peace and contentment that money cannot buy. They've been investing in forever long enough to see substantial returns on their faith investments.

The Insurance Policy of Faith

Perhaps the most practical reason to bet on forever is that faith provides the ultimate insurance policy. Lottery tickets offer no protection against life's uncertainties, but faith provides coverage for every possible scenario.

Consider the comprehensive coverage that faith provides:

- **Economic Protection:** Trust in God's provision during financial difficulties
- **Health Protection:** Peace and hope during illness and medical challenges
- **Relational Protection:** Forgiveness and reconciliation tools for relationship problems
- **Emotional Protection:** Joy and peace that don't depend on circumstances
- **Spiritual Protection:** Eternal security that transcends physical death
- **Purpose Protection:** Meaning and significance that can't be destroyed by external events

This isn't theoretical coverage—it's practical protection that works in real-world situations. I've seen this insurance policy pay out countless times in hospital rooms, family crises, job losses, and life transitions.

PRACTICAL EXERCISE: The Ultimate Lottery

Here's the ultimate irony: Faith is actually the ultimate lottery—except everyone who plays wins, the tickets are free, and the drawing has already happened.

Consider the "odds" of the faith lottery:

- Probability of God loving you: 100%
- Probability of forgiveness being available: 100%
- Probability of eternal life through Christ: 100%
- Probability of peace being available: 100%
- Probability of purpose being discoverable: 100%

The faith lottery has already been won by Jesus Christ, and He's sharing the winnings with everyone who wants them. You don't have to hope you'll win—you just have to accept the prize that's already been purchased for you.

The Decision Point

As this book concludes, you face the most important decision of your life—not just your financial life, but your eternal life. Will you continue betting on chance, or will you start betting on forever?

Here's what we've discovered together:

Lottery tickets promise external rescue through random chance Faith promises internal transformation through divine relationship

Lottery thinking creates anxiety about an uncertain future Faith thinking creates peace about a certain future

Lottery investments diminish over time through spending Faith investments compound over time through character development

Lottery wins benefit primarily the individual winner Faith wins benefit the believer and everyone they influence

Lottery jackpots end when the money is gone Faith jackpots continue forever

The choice is clear. But choosing requires action.

The Final Challenge

My final challenge to you isn't just to stop buying lottery tickets—though I hope you will. My final challenge is to start investing in forever with the same hope, excitement, and expectation that you once brought to lottery drawings.

Instead of checking lottery numbers every week, check your spiritual growth Instead of hoping for six matching numbers, hope for character that matches Christ's Instead of dreaming about what you'd do with lottery winnings, dream about what God could do through your surrendered life Instead of investing in chance, invest in the certainty of God's promises

The Forever Declaration

If you're ready to bet on forever, I invite you to make this declaration:

"I choose to bet on forever rather than chance. I will invest my time, money, hope, and energy in things that transcend this temporary world. I will seek first God's kingdom, knowing that everything else will be added to me. I will develop character that lasts beyond circumstances, relationships that endure beyond difficulty, and faith that survives every challenge. I will stop hoping for random rescue and start trusting in divine relationship. I declare that my ultimate security comes not from lucky numbers but from the One who numbers my days. I am betting everything on forever, and I know that everyone who makes this bet wins."

> **YOUR MIRROR QUESTION** *If you discovered today that you had exactly one year to live, what would matter most to you? What would you regret not investing in? What relationships would you prioritize? What legacy would you want to leave? Now ask yourself: Why wait? Why not start betting on what really matters—forever—today?*

The Winning Numbers

As I close this book, let me share the winning numbers that guarantee success:

John 3:16 - "For God so loved the world that he gave his one and only Son, that whoever believes in him shall not perish but have eternal life."

Romans 8:28 - "And we know that in all things God works for the good of those who love him, who have been called according to his purpose."

Philippians 4:19 - "And my God will meet all your needs according to the riches of his glory in Christ Jesus."

Matthew 6:33 - "But seek first his kingdom and his righteousness, and all these things will be given to you as well."

2 Corinthians 5:17 - "Therefore, if anyone is in Christ, the new creation has come: The old has gone, the new is here!"

These aren't lottery numbers—they're promise numbers. And unlike lottery numbers, these are guaranteed to win every time.

The Journey from Here

Your journey from lottery thinking to faith living starts with a single step: the decision to trust God more than you trust chance. From there, the path unfolds one day at a time, one choice at a time, one prayer at a time.

You'll have moments of doubt when the old lottery thinking resurfaces. You'll face circumstances that tempt you to look for external rescue rather than internal growth. You'll encounter people who think you're foolish for trusting God instead of hoping for luck.

But you'll also experience the peace that comes from knowing your future is secure in God's hands. You'll discover the joy of using your creativity to solve problems rather than hoping for random solutions. You'll build relationships based on genuine love rather than potential mutual benefit. You'll develop character that makes you valuable to others and confident in yourself.

Most importantly, you'll discover that the abundant life Jesus promised isn't something you win—it's something you live. Right now. Today. In your current circumstances with your present resources through your real relationships.

The Only Bet That Matters

The lottery industry wants you to believe that winning is about luck, timing, and random chance. The truth is that winning is about love, trust, and purposeful choice.

The only bet that really matters is the bet you make about God: Will you trust Him or trust chance? Will you believe His promises or hope for random rescue? Will you invest in forever or gamble on now?

I made my choice that night in 2019 when I threw away my last lottery ticket. Not because I'd given up hope for a better life, but because I'd discovered that the better life was already available through relationship with the God who creates, sustains, and redeems everything.

You have the same choice today.

You can keep buying tickets and hoping for lucky numbers. Or you can start living by faith and trusting in faithful promises.

You can keep betting on chance. Or you can start betting on forever.

The jackpot isn't waiting for you to win it. The jackpot is waiting for you to claim it.

The winning numbers aren't random. They're written in God's Word and revealed through His Son.

You don't need luck. You need love.

You don't need chance. You need choice.

You don't need lottery tickets. You need faith.

Bet on forever. It's the only guaranteed win.

And unlike the lottery, everyone who plays wins.

"For I know the plans I have for you," declares the Lord, "plans to prosper you and not to harm you, to give you hope and a future." ---*Jeremiah 29:11*

THE END

EPILOGUE

One Year Later: A Letter to My Readers

"Being confident of this, that he who began a good work in you will carry it on to completion until the day of Christ Jesus." —Philippians 1:6

Dear Friend,

It's been exactly one year since I threw away my last lottery ticket, and I wanted to share with you what has happened since I made the choice to bet on forever instead of chance.

I'm writing this letter from my piano bench at our church, where I've just finished practicing for tomorrow's service. The late afternoon sun is streaming through the stained glass windows, and I can hear my wife in the kitchen preparing dinner for the college students we've been mentoring this year. It's an ordinary Tuesday evening in our ordinary Connecticut home, and I've never felt richer.

Not because we've won any lottery. Not because we've experienced some dramatic financial windfall. But because we've discovered what you can only learn by living it: that a life invested in forever produces returns that begin immediately and continue eternally.

What We've Gained

Let me tell you what we've gained by giving up our "backup plan" to God:

Peace that makes no mathematical sense: Our financial situation is actually more challenging than it was a year ago. Healthcare costs have increased, inflation has affected our budget, and retirement is approaching faster than our savings account would prefer. But the anxiety that used to wake me up at 3 AM thinking about money has been replaced by a peace I can't explain. When you stop hoping for external rescue, you discover internal rest.

Creativity we didn't know we had: Remember how I mentioned that we're made in God's creative image? This year, that stopped being theology and became biography. My wife started a small business making and selling prayer journals that has connected her with women across the country. I've been teaching piano lessons to supplement our income, rediscovering the joy of music while helping others discover it for the first time. We're not just consuming solutions—we're creating them.

Relationships that money can't buy: When you stop focusing on what you might get, you start appreciating what you already have. Our marriage has deepened because we're no longer stressed about financial "what-ifs." Our relationships with our adult children have grown stronger because we're modeling contentment rather than anxiety. Our church family has become a source of joy rather than obligation because we're serving from gratitude rather than guilt.

Purpose that makes every day significant: I wake up each morning knowing that my life matters, not because of what I might accomplish or accumulate, but because of who I am in Christ and how I can serve others. Teaching nursing students, playing piano for worship, caring for patients, mentoring young people—every role feels like a calling rather than just a job.

What We've Lost

But I also want to be honest about what we've lost by giving up lottery thinking:

The illusion of quick fixes: We can no longer pretend that our problems might be solved by external intervention. When challenges arise, we have to face them with faith, creativity, and hard work rather than hoping for magical rescue.

The comfort of backup plans: There's something psychologically comforting about believing you have alternatives to God's provision. When you fully commit to trusting Him, you lose the safety net of "just in case" thinking.

The excitement of imaginary wealth: I'll admit there was a certain thrill in dreaming about what we'd do with lottery winnings. Giving up those fantasies meant accepting that our actual life, not our imaginary one, is where joy and purpose must be found.

The luxury of spiritual passivity: When you stop hoping that external circumstances will change your life, you have to take responsibility for spiritual growth, character development, and kingdom contribution.

As I reflect on these "losses," I realize they weren't losses at all—they were exchanges. We traded illusion for reality, fantasy for faith, passivity for purpose.

The Unexpected Discoveries

The most surprising part of this journey has been what we discovered that we never expected:

God's sense of humor: Who knew the Creator of the universe had such perfect timing and delightful irony? The week after I threw away my last lottery ticket, someone gave us a gift card to our favorite restaurant that we couldn't have afforded otherwise. The month we committed to tithing more generously, we received an unexpected tax refund. God seems to enjoy surprising people who trust Him.

The multiplication principle in action: Every skill we've developed this year has opened doors to other opportunities. Every person we've served has connected us to someone else who needed help. Every act of faith has increased our capacity for the next act of faith. Kingdom investment really does compound.

Community we didn't know existed: When you stop trying to solve your problems independently, you discover how many people are willing to help. Our church family, our neighbors, even colleagues at work have become sources of support and encouragement in ways we never experienced when we were focused on self-sufficiency.

Contentment that coexists with ambition: I used to think contentment meant giving up dreams and accepting mediocrity. Instead, I've learned that contentment provides the emotional stability needed to pursue meaningful goals without being driven by anxiety or greed.

The Ongoing Journey

This letter isn't written from a mountaintop of completed transformation. It's written from the valley of ongoing growth. We still face financial pressures. We still have to make difficult decisions. We still sometimes feel overwhelmed by life's complexities.

But we face these challenges differently now. Instead of our first thought being "How can we get lucky?" our first thought is "How can we trust God?" Instead of hoping for external intervention, we look for internal innovation. Instead of betting on chance, we're investing in character.

Some days are harder than others. Last month, when our car needed expensive repairs, I caught myself mentally calculating how that money could have bought lottery tickets and wondering if one of them might have been a winner. Old thought patterns die hard.

But then I remembered Harold Fletcher, the hospital janitor whose story I shared with you. Harold never had financial abundance, but he died wealthy in every way that matters. I remembered Mary Chen, who immigrated with $73 and built a legacy worth millions in impact. I remembered all the patients I've cared for who taught me that the richest people aren't always the ones with the most money.

A Message for You

If you're reading this book because you're struggling with lottery thinking, let me offer you some encouragement from someone who's walked this path:

It's worth it: Every day of freedom from lottery anxiety is better than any day of hoping for lottery rescue. The peace that comes from trusting God is more valuable than any jackpot.

It's possible: You don't need superhuman faith or perfect circumstances to make this transition. You just need to take the next right step and trust God to honor your movement toward Him.

It's not instant: Changing from lottery thinking to faith thinking is a process, not an event. Be patient with yourself as your mind and heart adjust to new patterns.

You're not alone: God specializes in helping people transition from dependence on chance to dependence on Him. Every story in Scripture is essentially about someone learning to trust God instead of circumstances.

The Invitation Continues

The invitation I extended throughout this book remains open: Stop betting on chance and start betting on forever. Stop hoping for random rescue and start trusting in divine relationship. Stop buying lottery tickets and start investing in kingdom reality.

But I want to extend an additional invitation: Join the community of people who are living this way. Find others who are choosing faith over chance, creativity over chance, service over self-focus. We need each other on this journey.

If this book has spoken to your heart, don't let the conversation end here. Talk to someone about what you've read. Share your own story of lottery thinking and faith growth. Become part of the solution by modeling a different way of living.

The Promise That Sustains

As I finish this letter, I want to leave you with the promise that has sustained my wife and me through this year of choosing faith over chance:

"And we know that in all things God works for the good of those who love him, who have been called according to his purpose" (Romans 8:28).

This promise doesn't mean that all things are good—some circumstances are difficult, painful, or challenging. But it does mean that God can work all things for good when we love Him and align our lives with His purposes.

The lottery promises that some things might work out well if you get lucky. God promises that all things will work out well when you trust Him.

The lottery asks you to hope for the best while preparing for disappointment. God asks you to prepare for blessing while trusting Him with the details.

Final Words

A year ago, I bought my last lottery ticket hoping that random numbers would change my life. Today, I can tell you with certainty that my life has been changed—not by chance, but by choice. Not by lucky numbers, but by faithful promises. Not by external circumstances, but by internal transformation.

The abundant life Jesus promised isn't waiting for you in some future lottery drawing. It's available right now, in your current circumstances, through relationship with the God who created you, redeems you, and calls you to participate in His ongoing creative work in the world.

You were made for more than hoping for luck. You were made for creating with faith. You were made for betting on forever.

The invitation stands: Will you join those of us who've discovered that God's favor is better than lucky numbers, that divine creativity is more reliable than random chance, and that eternal investment produces better returns than temporal gambling?

I pray that you will. And I pray that one year from today, you'll be writing your own letter about the transformative power of choosing faith over chance.

May you discover that the abundant life isn't something you win—it's something you live.

> *"Now to him who is able to do immeasurably more than we ask or imagine, according to his power that is at work within us, to him be glory in the church and in Christ Jesus throughout all generations for ever and ever! Amen."*
> *~Ephesians 3:20-21~*

APPENDICES

Appendix A: The 30-Day Faith Over Chance Challenge

Daily Actions for Breaking Lottery Thinking

Week 1: Recognition and Replacement

Day 1: Calculate how much you've spent on lottery tickets, scratch-offs, and gambling in the past year. Write this amount on a card and keep it visible.

Day 2: Open a "Kingdom Investment Fund" savings account. Deposit the amount you would normally spend on lottery tickets this week.

Day 3: List five problems in your life that you've been hoping lottery winnings would solve. For each problem, brainstorm three practical steps you could take today.

Day 4: Read Proverbs 21:5 - "The plans of the diligent lead to profit as surely as haste leads to poverty." Identify one area where you can be more diligent.

Day 5: Practice gratitude by listing ten things you already have that money can't buy.

Day 6: Complete the creativity assessment from Chapter 9. Identify your top three creative strengths.

Day 7: Reflect on the week. What was hardest about not buying lottery tickets? What was most surprising?

Week 2: Skill Development

Day 8: Choose one skill you want to develop over the next 90 days. Research free or low-cost ways to learn this skill.

Day 9: Spend 30 minutes learning something new related to your chosen skill.

Day 10: Find someone who has mastered your chosen skill and ask for advice or mentorship.

Day 11: Practice your new skill for at least 15 minutes. Document your progress.

Day 12: Read Matthew 25:14-30 (Parable of the Talents). Reflect on how you're stewarding your God-given abilities.

Day 13: Share what you're learning with someone else. Teaching reinforces learning.

Day 14: Assess your progress. What's working? What needs adjustment?

Week 3: Service and Generosity

Day 15: Identify one way you can serve others using your existing skills or resources.

Day 16: Volunteer for 2-3 hours with a local charity, church, or community organization.

Day 17: Use your "lottery money" to bless someone else - buy groceries for a neighbor, help a family in need, support a ministry.

Day 18: Practice random acts of kindness throughout the day. Notice how giving affects your mood.

Day 19: Read 2 Corinthians 9:6-8 about generous giving. Consider increasing your tithing or charitable giving.

Day 20: Connect with someone who's lonely - visit, call, or write a letter.

Day 21: Reflect on how serving others has impacted your perspective on your own needs.

Week 4: Faith Building

Day 22: Study one of God's promises in Scripture. Write it on a card and memorize it.

Day 23: Practice trusting God in a small decision. Before choosing, pray and seek His guidance.

Day 24: Share your testimony with someone - how has God been faithful in your life?

Day 25: Fast from one meal and spend that time in prayer, focusing on trusting God's provision.

Day 26: Read Philippians 4:11-13 about contentment. Practice being content with what you have today.

Day 27: Calculate how much you've saved in your Kingdom Investment Fund. Plan how to use it for kingdom purposes.

Day 28: Write a letter to yourself describing how you've changed over these 30 days.

Day 29: Plan your next 30 days. What kingdom investments will you make?

Day 30: Celebrate your transformation and commit to continued faith over chance living.

Appendix B: Scripture References for Faith-Based Living

Promises About God's Provision

- **Matthew 6:26** - "Look at the birds of the air; they do not sow or reap or store away in barns, and yet your heavenly Father feeds them. Are you not much more valuable than they?"
- **Philippians 4:19** - "And my God will meet all your needs according to the riches of his glory in Christ Jesus."
- **Psalm 23:1** - "The Lord is my shepherd, I lack nothing."
- **Psalm 84:11** - "For the Lord God is a sun and shield; the Lord bestows favor and honor; no good thing does he withhold from those whose walk is blameless."

Warnings About the Love of Money

- **1 Timothy 6:10** - "For the love of money is a root of all kinds of evil. Some people, eager for money, have wandered from the faith and pierced themselves with many griefs."

- **Hebrews 13:5** - "Keep your lives free from the love of money and be content with what you have, because God has said, 'Never will I leave you; never will I forsake you.'"
- **Matthew 6:24** - "No one can serve two masters. Either you will hate the one and love the other, or you will be devoted to the one and despise the other. You cannot serve both God and money."

Promises About Seeking God First

- **Matthew 6:33** - "But seek first his kingdom and his righteousness, and all these things will be given to you as well."
- **Jeremiah 29:13** - "You will seek me and find me when you seek me with all your heart."
- **Psalm 37:4** - "Take delight in the Lord, and he will give you the desires of your heart."

Encouragement for Faithful Stewardship

- **Luke 16:10** - "Whoever is faithful in very little is also faithful in much, and whoever is dishonest in very little is also dishonest in much."
- **1 Corinthians 4:2** - "Now it is required that those who have been given a trust must prove faithful."
- **Proverbs 3:9-10** - "Honor the Lord with your wealth, with the firstfruits of all your crops; then your barns

will be filled to overflowing, and your vats will brim over with new wine."

Appendix C: Practical Tools for Kingdom Investment

The Kingdom Investment Calculator

Step 1: Calculate Your Lottery/Gambling Expenses

- Weekly lottery tickets: $____
- Monthly scratch-offs: $____
- Annual casino visits: $____
- Online gambling: $____
- **Total Annual Gambling Expense: $____**

Step 2: Calculate Potential Kingdom Investments With your annual gambling expense, you could:

- Take ____ college courses at $150 each
- Buy ____ books for personal development at $15 each
- Fund ____ hours of professional coaching at $50/hour
- Support ____ missionaries at $50/month each
- Provide ____ meals for homeless individuals at $5 each

Step 3: Project 10-Year Kingdom ROI If you invested your gambling money in skills development:

- Year 1: New skills acquired
- Year 3: Increased income potential

- Year 5: Enhanced career opportunities
- Year 10: Compounded benefits to yourself and others

The Weekly Faith Investment Plan

Sunday: Spiritual Investment (1-2 hours)

- Worship service attendance
- Scripture study and prayer
- Spiritual goal setting for the week

Monday: Character Investment (30 minutes daily)

- Focus on one character quality (patience, kindness, integrity)
- Practice this quality in daily interactions
- Reflect on growth and areas for improvement

Tuesday: Skill Investment (45 minutes)

- Work on developing one practical skill
- Take online courses, read instructional materials, or practice

Wednesday: Relationship Investment (1 hour)

- Invest in family relationships
- Connect with friends or mentors
- Build community connections

Thursday: Service Investment (1-2 hours)

- Volunteer work or community service
- Help neighbors or church members

- Support local charities or causes

Friday: Financial Investment (30 minutes)

- Review and plan finances according to kingdom principles
- Make charitable contributions
- Plan future kingdom investments

Saturday: Rest and Reflection (Variable time)

- Sabbath rest and family time
- Reflect on the week's investments
- Plan improvements for next week

The Creative Problem-Solving Framework

Step 1: Define the Problem Clearly

- What exactly needs to be solved?
- Who is affected by this problem?
- What resources are currently available?

Step 2: Pray for Wisdom

- Ask God for creative solutions
- Seek His guidance on the best approach
- Trust that He has equipped you to find answers

Step 3: Brainstorm Multiple Solutions

- Generate at least 10 possible approaches
- Don't judge ideas initially - just create
- Ask others for input and perspectives

Step 4: Evaluate Options Using Kingdom Criteria

- Which solution serves others best?
- Which develops your character most?
- Which aligns with biblical principles?
- Which creates the most positive long-term impact?

Step 5: Implement with Faith

- Choose the best solution and act
- Trust God to multiply your efforts
- Be willing to adjust as you learn

Step 6: Share and Multiply

- Document what you learn
- Teach others your solution
- Look for ways to expand the impact

Appendix D: Frequently Asked Questions

Q: Is it wrong to ever hope for financial improvement?

A: Absolutely not! God wants us to experience provision and even prosperity. The issue isn't hoping for financial improvement—it's depending on random chance rather than trusting God's provision and developing our abilities.

Q: What if I've already won money from the lottery? Does that make me a bad Christian?

A: Past lottery wins don't determine your spiritual standing with God. The question is: moving forward, will you trust lottery luck or divine provision? Use any past winnings wisely and commit to kingdom investment going forward.

Q: How do I know if God wants me to be wealthy?

A: God's desire for your prosperity is less about the amount of money you have and more about your character, generosity, and impact. Seek first His kingdom, develop your God-given abilities, and trust Him with the financial results.

Q: What about investing in stocks or starting a business? Isn't that also risky?

A: There's a difference between calculated risk based on research and wisdom versus random chance based on luck.

Stocks and businesses involve research, strategy, and skill development. Lottery tickets involve pure chance.

Q: I live in poverty. Isn't the lottery my only hope for a better life?

A: The lottery actually preys on people in poverty and statistically makes their situations worse. Focus instead on developing skills, education, and character that create sustainable pathways out of poverty. Many resources are available for low-income skill development.

Q: What if my spouse/family members still play the lottery?

A: Focus on your own transformation first. Live as an example of faith-based provision rather than lecturing others. Share this book if appropriate, but let your changed life be the primary testimony.

Q: How do I overcome the temptation to buy "just one more ticket"?

A: Remember that each ticket represents a vote of no confidence in God's provision. Redirect that money immediately to your kingdom investment fund. Have accountability partners who know about your commitment.

Appendix E: Recommended Resources for Continued Growth

Books on Faith and Finances

- *The Total Money Makeover* by Dave Ramsey
- *Your Money or Your Life* by Vicki Robin
- *The Treasure Principle* by Randy Alcorn
- *Master Your Money* by Ron Blue
- *God Owns It All* by R.G. LeTourneau

Books on Discovering Your Calling

- *Strengthsfinder 2.0* by Tom Rath
- *What Color Is Your Parachute?* by Richard N. Bolles
- *The Purpose Driven Life* by Rick Warren
- *Designing Your Life* by Bill Burnett and Dave Evans

Books on Character Development

- *The Seven Habits of Highly Effective People* by Stephen Covey
- *Mere Christianity* by C.S. Lewis
- *The Practice of the Presence of God* by Brother Lawrence
- *Celebration of Discipline* by Richard Foster

Online Resources

- **Crown Financial Ministries** (crown.org) - Biblical financial principles
- **Ramsey Solutions** (ramseyschool.com) - Financial education
- **Coursera/edX** - Free and low-cost skill development courses
- **VolunteerMatch** (volunteermatch.org) - Service opportunities
- **SCORE** (score.org) - Free business mentoring
- Organizations for Gambling Recovery
- Gamblers Anonymous (gamblersanonymous.org)
- National Council on Problem Gambling (ncpgambling.org)
- Focus on the Family - Christian counseling resources.

Appendix F: Prayer Guide for Faith Over Chance Living

Daily Prayers

Morning Prayer for Provision "Father, I commit this day to You. Help me trust Your provision rather than seeking my own schemes. Give me eyes to see opportunities You've placed before me and wisdom to steward them well. May I seek first Your kingdom today. Amen."

Prayer Before Financial Decisions "Lord, I bring this financial decision to You. Help me choose according to Your wisdom rather than my fears or greed. May this choice honor You and serve others. I trust Your provision and guidance. Amen."

Evening Prayer of Gratitude "Thank You, God, for Your faithfulness today. Help me recognize how You've provided, protected, and guided me. Forgive me for any moments when I trusted chance more than Your character. Prepare my heart for tomorrow's opportunities to trust You. Amen."

Weekly Prayers

Sunday: Prayer for Spiritual Growth "Father, grow my faith this week. Help me trust You more deeply and serve You more faithfully. May my life be a testimony to Your goodness and provision."

Wednesday: Prayer for Wisdom "Lord, grant me wisdom in all my decisions this week. Help me see clearly, choose wisely, and act according to Your will rather than my impulses."

Friday: Prayer for Generosity "God, make me generous with the resources You've entrusted to me. Help me give freely of my time, talents, and treasure for Your kingdom purposes."

Prayers for Specific Situations

When Tempted to Buy Lottery Tickets "Lord, I'm feeling the pull toward lottery thinking again. Remind me that You are my provider and my hope. Help me redirect this money toward kingdom investment. Strengthen my faith in Your provision. Amen."

When Facing Financial Pressure "Father, I'm feeling financial stress and the temptation to seek quick solutions. Help me trust Your timing and Your provision. Show me creative ways to address these challenges. Give me peace as I wait on You. Amen."

When Seeing Others Win or Succeed "God, help me rejoice with others without feeling diminished. Remind me that Your blessings aren't limited and that You have good plans for me too. Keep my heart free from envy and full of trust. Amen."

Acknowledgements

This book could not have come into being without the love, encouragement, and support of so many people whose presence has shaped my life and work.

First, I thank my mother, **Alder R. Davis**. Your prayers, strength, and vision are the very heartbeat of this project. You not only raised sons but also instilled in us the values of faith, perseverance, and honor. This book is as much your story as it is mine. Your encouragement through every season of my life continues to remind me of the power of unconditional love.

To my father, the late **Edward L. Davis, Sr.**: though you left us too soon, your example of sacrifice, integrity, and quiet strength remains a compass in my life. You set a standard for what it means to be a man of character, and I will forever honor the foundation you laid for our family.

To my late brother, **Jeffery Davis**: your spirit still echoes in my heart. You continually reminded us to keep our faith in God, and that encouragement remains alive in every page of this work. Your wisdom and faith walk beside me still.

I also wish to acknowledge my brothers, each of whom has shaped me in unique ways. From **Eddie's** leadership to **Kevin's** zeal, **Jonathan's** loyalty, **Troy's** transformation, **Jason's** brilliance, and the **memory of Jeffery's** deep spirituality—

each of you is a vital part of this story. Together, we have carried forward the legacy entrusted to us.

To my wife, **Arvita**, and my children— **Edwin, DJ, Daria, Darius, Demitrius, and Nadia**—thank you for your patience and understanding as I poured countless hours into writing. Your love and encouragement gave me strength when the work felt overwhelming.

To my extended family and friends, who reminded me that this story matters and urged me to finish it: thank you for your voices, your laughter, and your prayers.

Finally, I acknowledge the grace of **God**, without whom none of this would be possible. Every chapter, every word, and every testimony in these pages is a reflection of His faithfulness. May this book honor Him and inspire others to trust in His plan.

About the Author

Elder D. Christopher, Sr. is a man who has lived on both sides of faith and chance. A healthcare worker and registered nurse for nearly four decades and an ordained minister, he has witnessed firsthand the power of belief, the fragility of human hope, and the quiet dangers of putting trust in "backup plans" rather than in God.

From his early years, Elder Christopher learned that faith was not meant to be a gamble but a foundation. Yet, like many, he once struggled with the lure of chance thinking — believing that a lottery ticket or a "lucky break" might change everything. Those personal battles now fuel his writing. His candid honesty allows readers to see themselves in his story, while his spiritual clarity points them toward a life anchored in God's promises.

Beyond his professional and ministerial callings, Elder Christopher is a husband, father, and musician who serves faithfully in his church and community. He is passionate about helping people discover the richness of Kingdom living — not by waiting for odds to shift in their favor, but by walking confidently in the abundance God has already made available.

With *Faith vs The Lottery: A Journey From Backup Plans to Divine Abundance,* he invites readers into a conversation that is both urgent and timeless: stop gambling with chance, and start investing in the only guarantee that never fails — the Word of God.

www.ingramcontent.com/pod-product-compliance
Lightning Source LLC
Chambersburg PA
CBHW070140100426
42743CB00013B/2774